André F. Raine | Helen Raine
Jason Raine | Jill Raine

A Guide to the Island's Wildlife

Bermuda's Top 10: A Guide to the Island's Wildlife
All text, photographs and illustrations © 2015 André F. Raine, Helen Raine,
Jason Raine and Jill Raine, except as noted below:

Diamondback Terrapin © 2015 Mark Outerbridge
Painted Lady Butterfly © 2015 Vickie Cole
Red Admiral, Blue Dasher Dragonfly © 2015 Jay Cossey
Seaside Morning Glory © 2015 Yuki Reiss
Bermuda Skink, Grey Catbird, Bermuda White-eyed Vireo © 2015 Tim White
American Cockroach © 2013 Smuaya | Dreamstime.com
Northern Cardinal © 2012 Mirceax | Dreamstime.com
Cabbage White © Pnwnature | Dreamstime.com

"there's just a sense" © 1992 David F. Raine

Printed by Total Print Solutions, Bermuda

ISBN: 978-1-927750-81-0

First printing, 2015

Published by Pompano Publications
21 Convict Bay Lane, St. George's, Bermuda GE05

Dedicated with all our love
to David F. Raine
(1941-2004)

CREDITS

Research and Text
André F. Raine and Helen Raine

Illustration and Design
Jason Raine

Photography and Watercolours
Jill Raine

Poetry
David F. Raine

Additional Photography
André F. Raine | Green Turtle, Hawksbill Turtle,
Humpback Whale, Bottlenose Dolphin, Giant Centipede,
Bird-of-Paradise Flower
Mark Outerbridge | Diamondback Terrapin
Vickie Cole (ObsessionWithButterflies.com) | Painted Lady Butterfly
Jay Cossey (PhotographsFromNature.com) | Red Admiral, Blue Dasher Dragonfly
Yuki Reiss | Seaside Morning Glory
Tim White | Bermuda Skink, Grey Catbird, Bermuda
White-eyed Vireo

Special thanks to all of our contributors.

Thanks to Paul Pethick for his recommendations.

TABLE OF CONTENTS

Use this checklist to record where you've been and what you've seen — and what still needs to be tracked down before you leave!

INTRODUCTION

*I*f you're reading this book, the chances are you're in Bermuda already or heading here soon. Well lucky you; this fascinating group of low-lying, linked islands in the middle of the Atlantic Ocean has lush vegetation, white-roofed houses, pink beaches and turquoise seas. It's the archetypal tropical island holiday destination and despite its small size (only 21 square miles), it has some phenomenal wildlife too.

It won't take you long to spot some of the island's iconic species and that's where the Bermuda Top Ten comes in. It's a crash course on the common birds, plants and animals that you're likely to find here. We will explain which sea creatures you are going to float past when you're snorkelling; what that famous yellow bird's real name is; how to spot a glowing green Bermuda Fire Worm; and the best places to look for all of these amazing creatures and plants.

We have grouped the wildlife together to make it easy to navigate to the crab that's scuttling past your beach towel or the gorgeous flower that just caught your eye. Each species is represented by a photograph or drawing showing its most distinctive features, followed by a description detailing how to identify it from other similar species.

We will tell you whether the species is a native or endemic (found here and nowhere else); these are particularly fun to track down because this might be your only chance to see them. We have a lot of introduced species on the island too, brought here by humans. Some are lovely and benign; others are causing all sorts of trouble for native wildlife. These conservation challenges are also discussed within the pages of this book.

We hope that with the aid of this pocket guide, you will be better able to appreciate the natural beauty of the island and put a name to some of our non-human residents. Bermuda has so much to offer and we hope you find the time to enjoy the wildlife of our beaches, parks, oceans and woodlands as much as we do!

-André, Jill, Jason and Helen

BERMUDA

ATLANTIC
OCEAN

Royal Naval
Dockyard

Arboretum —

PEMBROKE

Somerset
Village

City of
HAMILTON

VII

SANDY'S

VIII

Paget
Marsh

Hog
Bay
Park

X

PAGET

SOUTHAMPTON

WARWICK

IX

South Shore Park

Horseshoe
Bay

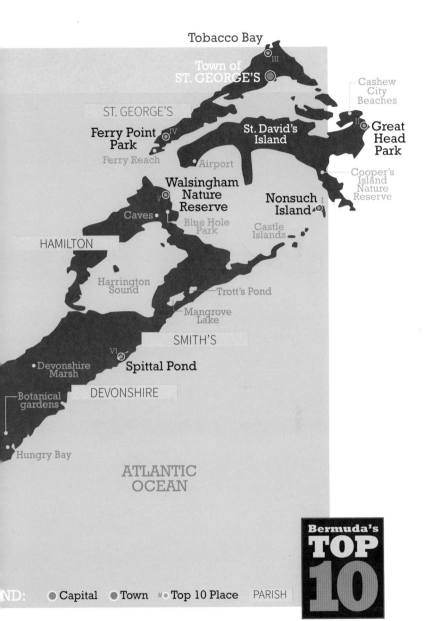

Tobacco Bay

Town of
ST. GEORGE'S

III

Cashew
City
Beaches

ST. GEORGE'S

Ferry Point
Park

IV

St. David's
Island

II

Great
Head
Park

Ferry Reach

Airport

Cooper's
Island
Nature
Reserve

Walsingham
Nature
Reserve

V

Nonsuch
Island

I

Caves

Blue Hole
Park

Castle
Islands

HAMILTON

Harrington
Sound

Trott's Pond

Mangrove
Lake

SMITH'S

Spittal Pond

VI

Devonshire
Marsh

DEVONSHIRE

Botanical
gardens

Hungry Bay

ATLANTIC
OCEAN

Bermuda's
TOP
10

ND: ● Capital ● Town # ● Top 10 Place PARISH

1

HABITATS

Introduction

*B*ermuda's habitats have been shaped by its long history of isolation, way out in the Atlantic Ocean. Originally they consisted of forests of Bermuda Cedar and Palmetto, dotted with marshes and fringed by mangroves and pristine beaches. The appearance of humans in the 1500s (sailors left pigs on the island as a future source of food for emergencies), and the subsequent shipwreck of the Sea Venture in 1609, changed Bermuda's landscapes forever. New species were introduced, marshes were drained, forests were cut down to build ships and agriculture began.

Although the habitats of today are generally very different from what you would have seen in the pre-settlement period, one can still catch glimpses of the 'old Bermuda' in some of the protected Nature Reserves around the island. Our beaches and the sea are probably the least changed; they are well protected and many of those long expanses of pink sand and turquoise waters would be familiar to the exhausted survivors who washed up onto Bermuda's shores after their famous shipwreck.

Regardless of the changes, Bermuda's habitats are a fascinating composite of sea, coast, woodland and marshland. So take a break from relaxing to do some exploring; beachcombing and snorkelling along the shorelines and protected bays can be very rewarding. You should also venture inland to explore our shady woodlands, still beautiful despite the new composition of species, or our marshes like Spittal Pond and Paget Marsh, which have been lovingly restored (almost) to their former glory.

We have also included several man-made habitats in this chapter; gardens, farmland, golf courses and towns. These areas might not immediately spring to mind as important wildlife habitats, but they each have their own flora and fauna and are certainly places in which you'll be spending some time during your stay.

Sea I

You are never more than a mile from the sea, no matter where you go in Bermuda; it's the largest habitat we have. Our tiny islands rose out of the ocean floor as a volcanic eruption over 100 million years ago, so for hundreds of miles around, there's some deep, deep water out there with an incredibly diverse array of inhabitants.

At Challenger Bank, the drop-off plunges down for fathoms, and huge pelagic fish, such as Blue Marlin and Wahoo, prowl these deep, blue expanses. Take a boat trip off Bermuda's shores and if you're lucky, you might also see some of our favourite sea mammals such as Bottlenose Dolphins or the migratory population of Humpback Whales.

For snorkelers and scuba divers, we also have some of the most northerly coral reefs in the Atlantic Ocean, which add incredible splashes of colour to the ocean blue. The reefs protect the islands from being swept away by the great rolling waves of the sea – a good reason not to stand on or touch these fragile structures as they can die when they are damaged. In the calm shallows adjacent to docks and beaches, you'll find brightly coloured reef fish darting in and out of the corals while moray eels and lobsters peer cautiously out of natural crevices. Children in particular will get a kick out of exploring these areas and looking for the profusion of wildlife in the protected waters.

II Beaches

Think of beaches in Bermuda and you immediately envisage huge, curving expanses of pink sand, or perhaps one of the many hidden gems tucked into coves and bays throughout the island. Add a sprinkling of tourists (and the occasional bright red form of a sunbather who forgot to apply suntan lotion!) reclining on beach-chairs or sprawled out on towels, and you could be forgiven for thinking that that's all there is to beaches – sunbathing and swimming. However, beaches are also important habitats for a wide range of species. Atlantic Ghost Crabs skitter in front of advancing waves; the small, grey-feathered forms of migratory Sanderlings poke amongst the debris washed up by the sea; and a variety of plant species colonise the adjacent dune systems, including Bermuda's national flower, the Bermudiana.

Tobacco Bay and Horseshoe Bay are good places to start exploring. If you are lucky enough to visit some of the beaches on the Castle Islands, you may also see our endemic Bermuda Skink scavenging for morsels washed up by the sea.

Shoreline III

Away from the famous beaches, our shoreline gets rocky and windswept, with crumbling cliffs dropping down to the sea below. On more gently sloping coastal areas, rock pools contain a host of treasures waiting to be discovered, such as tiny fish, transparent shrimp, fast-moving crabs, the spiny forms of sea urchins and the limpet-like Chiton.

The shoreline is one of the best places to view the graceful White-tailed Tropicbirds when they arrive on the island to breed (late February to late October). Or, as dusk settles, you can seek out the Yellow-crowned Night Herons; they will be stalking the rocks, bashing hapless land crabs to bits on convenient rocky anvils.

The vegetation on the shoreline, like that of the beach, has evolved to protect itself against incessant sea-spray and the onslaught of the elements. It includes species such as Bay Grape, Sea Ox-eye and Buttonwood. The rocky coastline of Spittal Pond is worth visiting with its strange checkerboard geological formation. As an added bonus, this is also a good place to spot a Bermuda Skink, if you're lucky.

IV Mangroves

Bermuda's mangroves are the most northerly in the Atlantic. Once covering large areas of the country, they are now reduced to small pockets scattered about the island (something which has sadly been seen throughout the world as this important ecosystem is destroyed for development). This habitat plays many important roles in Bermuda, protecting us against storm surges and wave action, as well as being a key nursery ground for many species of reef fish.

Only two species of mangrove are found in Bermuda; the Red Mangrove and the Black Mangrove. The habitat they create is a great place to watch birds; during migration it provides food and shelter for a range of species, such as warblers and vireos. You might also see several types of shells and crabs, including the rare Giant Land Crab which is native to Bermuda and can grow over four inches long and weigh as much as 17 ounces. With its impressive front claws, one being larger than the other, this crab is definitely in the 'look but don't touch' category!

To find pockets of mangroves along the coast, look in areas such as Walsingham Nature Reserve, as well as in a small number of ponds on the island including Spittal Pond and Paget Marsh.

Woodlands V

The majority of woodlands found in Bermuda today are a completely different ecosystem than the pre-settlement era. In ages past, these forests would have been dominated by Bermuda Cedar and Bermuda Palmetto, along with other local species such as Bermuda Olivewood and Yellow Wood. Unfortunately, human settlement resulted in large-scale clearance of these woods to build houses and ships. The final nail in the coffin was the appearance of the cedar blight in the mid-1940s, carried by scale insects on ornamental junipers. This disease rapidly killed off the vast majority of these endemic trees, with the result that the character of Bermudian woodlands was fundamentally changed forever. There are still a few areas where one can get a feel for the original woodlands of Bermuda, such as the interior of Nonsuch Island. However, mostly, you will encounter introduced tree species, such as Allspice, Surinam Cherry, Fiddlewood, Brazil Pepper and Chinese Fan Palm.

Despite the conservation doom and gloom, walking through woodlands makes for a pleasant afternoon and provides a good way to become acquainted with some of our bird species, such as the Bermuda White-eyed Vireo, Gray Catbird and Northern Cardinal. You can easily spot several of our introduced Anolis lizard species, sunning themselves on the trees, while both the Silk Spider and the Spiny Orbweaver Spider should also be readily visible.

VI Marshes

In pre-settlement times, much of Bermuda's low-lying, inland areas consisted of freshwater peat marshes. These damp, sun-dappled areas contained a high diversity of native and endemic plant species and were home to a multitude of birds and invertebrates. Over the years, development, garbage dumping and landfill have done away with much of this habitat. However, due to inspired conservation work, some fine examples still remain to show what Bermuda was really like when the first settlers crawled out of the surf onto virgin land.

Plant species, such as Wax Myrtle, Bermuda Cedar, Bermuda Palmetto, Sawgrass and a range of sedges and ferns, can all be found in these boggy areas. These in turn provide refuge for waterbirds, migrating birds or bats and a wide variety of insects, including dragonflies and damselflies. Meanwhile, under the more saline murky waters, our endemic Killifish (small fish that look like guppies) flit about, ever wary of predators.

Paget Marsh and Devonshire Marsh are prime examples of this habitat and are well worth a visit.

Caves VII

Bermuda has one of the highest concentrations of caves in the world, home to a host of endemic species. They were formed by the ever-so-slow process of water dissolving, over thousands of years, the limestone base of Bermuda. A journey into the caves will take you deep underground, past strange formations, including stalactites (from the cave roof downwards) and stalagmites (from the cave floor upwards) and underground lakes.

For the sheer spectacle, a trip to some of the more well known 'tourist attraction' caves - such as Crystal Cave and Fantasy Cave - is well worth it. But it's also fun to (cautiously) explore some of the lesser-known grottos on the island; try Walsingham Nature Reserve and Blue Hole Park where caves are scattered about the interior, their mouths festooned with ferns and their blue, watery depths reflecting wavering images of stalactites.

There are a range of endemic shrimp, copepods and isopods found in Bermuda's cave systems, the vast majority of which are exceedingly rare and often restricted to a single cave. An example is the Bermuda Cave Shrimp, a miniscule little beast discovered in 1985. It measures only ⅛ of an inch, has no pigment and is blind. It spends its entire life scudding around the inky black waters of caves such as those in Tucker's Town. It goes without saying that caves are exceptionally fragile ecosystems and need to be treated with care and respect. We also strongly recommend you do not go too far into any of the caves as it can be very hard to find your way back out again!

VIII Gardens and Farmland

Bermudians pride themselves on their gardens and they are often important areas for our native and endemic flora and fauna. David Raine, whose poem is featured at the end of the book, spent countless hours planting and pruning a verdant mini-rainforest of loquat, banana, coconut palms, hibiscus and other flowering shrubs in our own backyard. Birds attracted to all this greenery include natives such as Eastern Bluebirds and migrant warblers, while the raucous calls of kiskadees sound from overhanging palm trees. Many gardens have specimens of Bermuda Cedars and Bermuda Palmettos, thus acting as an important refuge for these species. Anolis lizards scurry about in the trees and you can find the occasional Marine Toad lurking in the cool, damp spaces behind plant pots. It is these gardens which give Bermuda such a 'green' feel and tastefully hide the fact that the country is heavily developed. The most splendid example is the Botanical Gardens in Paget; take time to wander about its grounds.

While gardens make up much of the Bermudian green space, agricultural areas are also an important habitat on the island. These pockets of farmland provide a wealth of habitat for our flora and fauna, especially in farms with limited use of pesticides and herbicides. Many fields have been in continuous use for hundreds of years and the fertile soil still yields delicious produce; you'll see it for sale in our local markets.

Golf Courses IX

Golf courses are an important refuge for many species, particularly birds. This is because they have a range of habitats, with their vast greens, scattered shrubs and trees, water features and sand traps.

Eastern Bluebirds, a native species that is something of a conservation success story in Bermuda, thrive here and readily utilise the nest boxes mounted at the edge of the courses. During migration, warblers and vireos can be found in the patches of woodland and mangrove, while swallows and martins flit overhead catching insects. Meanwhile, waders congregate on any flooded areas to poke and prod with their bills. Sadly, the (often heavy) use of pesticides and fertilisers can detract from this environment, particularly for the aquatic habitats within. Please remember - if you're looking for wildlife on the greens, make sure you also keep an eye out for fast-moving, small white balls!

X Urban Areas

The ultimate in human habitats, our urban areas cover the island in a kaleidoscope of pastel-coloured houses and gleaming white roofs (the roofs are used to catch rainwater as there are no sources of drinking water on the island). Our towns are mainly of interest for cultural, architectural and historical reasons. Walking around 'Ye Olde Towne' of St. George's, for example, will transport you back in time several centuries.

Wildlife has adapted to, and invaded, every corner of the urban landscape as well. Most of the species you can see in our towns are introduced. They include the squabbling ranks of House Sparrows and European Starlings that nip in to grab the remains of sandwiches. In the evenings, close inspections of window sills may reveal the cause of all of the monotonous 'beep beep beeps' that keep some tourists awake – the Lesser Antillean Whistling Frog. Perhaps less pleasingly, you might hear the sudden whirring of American Cockroach wings. It is a remarkable testament to the resilience of nature, that even our most heavily altered landscapes can still contain a profusion of wildlife.

2

BIRDS

Introduction

*B*eing such a small, isolated and densely populated island, Bermuda only has 23 resident breeding bird species. Of these, two are endemic to the island (with one of these being an endemic sub-species), meaning they are found here and nowhere else in the world. Unfortunately, our other endemic species are now long extinct, as is sadly the way with many island species adapted to life without humans. The birds you are most likely to encounter when wandering around the island have usually been introduced by humans. The commonest are the House Sparrow, European Starling, Great Kiskadee and Feral Pigeon.

Despite having a relatively small number of breeding bird species, Bermuda's avifauna is swelled dramatically every year by the appearance of a host of migrant species and those blown far off course by storms. These birds pass through the island on the way to and from breeding and wintering grounds. On southwards migration, some individuals stop and spend the winter here, rather than travel onwards. It is an exciting time to look for birds as you might spot a wide variety of gulls, waterfowl, waders and passerine species, many of which will be familiar to North American visitors. This influx of migrant species has led to the island list totalling over 360 species, so a walk through Bermuda in the spring, autumn or winter can turn up a variety of interesting sightings. In this chapter, however, we have mainly discussed the common resident species (with a few exceptions), as it is these that you are more likely to see whatever time of year you visit the island.

Of course we can't talk about Bermuda's birds without mentioning the incredible conservation success story of one of the world's rarest seabirds – the legendary Bermuda Cahow, historically known as the "Devil Bird". Once thought extinct, this beautiful bird is making a comeback on the island through a lot of dedication and effort. It really is a Bermudian specialty and a bird held close to our hearts. They are extremely difficult to see as they spend most of their lives at sea and only return to Bermuda to breed, but you may be lucky if you try spotting them out at sea during their breeding season.

Bermuda Cahow I
Pterodroma cahow

Endemic

Rare

Alternative name(s) Bermuda Petrel
Length 15in (38cm)
When Breeds in Bermuda between October and June
Where Early evening out at sea off the Castle Islands
Habitat Breeds on offshore islets, feeds far out at sea

Our National Bird, the endemic Bermuda Cahow is a small petrel species that once nested throughout the island in its millions. Early settlers found this species to be very unwary, as they had evolved on an isolated island with no land predators. This unfortunately meant that they were easy to catch for food, leading to their rapid extermination. The last known birds were wiped out by introduced rats and wild hogs. For centuries the species was presumed extinct until the exciting re-discovery of a few pairs in 1951 on an offshore island. Through the painstaking work of conservationists such as David Wingate and Jeremy Madeiros, the Cahow finally topped the 100 breeding pairs mark in 2012. It is a beautiful dark grey and white seabird which returns to the island at night only during the breeding season. As of 2009 the Cahow is now once again nesting on Nonsuch Island after an innovative translocation and social attraction project.

II White-tailed Tropicbird
Phaethon lepturus

Native (breeding visitor)   Common

Alternative name(s) Longtail
Length 32in (80cm)
When February-October
Where St David's Head, Castle Islands, Spittal Pond
Habitat Shoreline, offshore islets, at sea

The White-tailed Tropicbird, or 'Longtail', is one of Bermuda's best-loved native sea birds and is something of a Bermudian icon, heralding the arrival of spring. It only comes to Bermuda to breed, being present from late February to late October. During the peak summer months, this species is a regular feature of island life, gracefully wheeling past our coasts and shorelines.

It is easily recognised by its immaculate white and black plumage, bright orange-red bill and elongated central tail feathers (which earn it its local name). Although still fairly common, it is under increasing pressure from introduced feral pigeons, which compete with it for nesting areas, and predation from cats and rats. There are an estimated 2,500-3,000 pairs nesting on Bermuda, making up around half of the North Atlantic breeding population.

Yellow-crowned Night Heron **III**
Nyctanassa violacea

Native (reintroduced)

Frequent

Alternative name(s)   None
Length   24in (61cm)
When   Year-round
Where   Spittal Pond, Paget Marsh
Habitat   Mangroves, pond edges, swamps, shoreline

The Yellow-crowned Night Heron was re-introduced to the island in the mid-1970s after being eliminated in early colonial days. It is a medium-sized heron, far smaller than the Great Blue Heron (*Ardea herodias*) which you may also encounter and which is a common migrant to the island. This night heron is easy to identify, with adults resplendent in their pale grey plumage and conspicuous black and white head with yellow crown. Juveniles on the other hand are a dull brown colour, extensively flecked with white. Breeding colonies are found in some of our mangroves and swamps and the birds are often seen along the coast, busy dismembering red land crabs on the jagged rocks.

IV Moorhen
Gallinula chloropus

Native (migrant)

Frequent

Alternative name(s) Common Gallinule
Length 13in (33cm)
When Year-round
Where Spittal Pond, Pembroke Marsh, Paget Marsh
Habitat Ponds, marshes, swamps, golf courses

Another resident breeding bird, the moorhen is a stocky, chicken-like bird that inhabits ponds, marshes and swampy areas. Adults have a chocolate brown back, slaty grey breast and conspicuous bright red frontal shield above the yellow-tipped bill. This easily sets it apart from another common resident, the American Coot (*Fulica americana*), which is structurally similar but has a white frontal shield and bill.

Moorhens move easily around muddy expanses on their strangely lobed feet and feed on aquatic vegetation. They are a common sight in wetland areas around the island, as well as on golf courses near water features and flooded areas.

Mourning Dove V
Zenaida macroura

Native (migrant)

Common

Alternative name(s) None
Length 12in (31cm)
When Year-round
Where Island-wide
Habitat Woodlands, farmland, gardens, parks

One of our two resident, breeding dove species, the Mourning Dove is a common sight on the island and is found in many habitats. It is a relatively recent arrival to the island (with the first breeding record from the 1950s) but migrated here naturally and was not introduced to Bermuda. It can be easily distinguished from our second dove species, the Common Ground-Dove (*Columbina passerina*) by its elegant, slender appearance and upright posture. The Common Ground-Dove on the other hand, is a small, dumpy bird which can often be spotted, in pairs, trotting along the path in front of you. The only other bird with which you might confuse the doves is the feral pigeon but this is a larger bird, of varying colours, and mainly found in larger flocks. The Mourning Dove gets its name from the plaintive call that it makes.

VI Great Kiskadee
Pitangus sulphuratus

Introduced

Common

Alternative name(s) Yellow Bird
Length 9.5in (24cm)
When Year-round
Where Island-wide
Habitat Everywhere!

One of our most abundant and conspicuous birds, the Great Kiskadee was introduced from Trinidad. It is easily recognised by its bright yellow breast, black and white face and '*Kis-ka-dee*' call. Probably one of the first bird species you will see on your visit, it is often seen perched on telephone wires or calling from trees in gardens, woodlands and towns. This species is a prime example of how *not* to carry out a biological control program. It was originally brought to the island to control lizards, which had been introduced to the island to control cockroaches and flies, which had mistakenly been introduced to the island by people. Unfortunately, instead of controlling introduced lizards, kiskadees also opted to prey upon the nestlings of native birds and our endemic skink, making them a serious threat to many of our native species. It's also the subject of a familiar island song, '*Yellow Bird.*'

Eastern Bluebird VII
Sialia sialis

Native

Frequent

Alternative name(s)   None
Length   7in (18cm)
When   Year-round
Where   Try the larger golf courses
Habitat   Woodlands, gardens, golf courses, parks

Another distinctive bird, the Eastern Bluebird is a native breeding species on the island. Often seen on golf courses and agricultural land, the males of this attractive species are cobalt blue on the back and tail and have reddish-brown throats and breasts. Females follow the same general patterning but are somewhat duller in colouration; newly fledged birds are heavily speckled. Like the Longtail, they are under pressure from introduced species, particularly the House Sparrow, which out-competes them for nest holes. An intensive conservation program, in the form of hundreds of special nest boxes, received widespread local support and has succeeded in helping to reverse their precipitous decline on the island. You can often spot these boxes on the many golf courses around the island.

VIII Grey Catbird
Dumetella carolinensis

Native

Frequent

Alternative name(s) None
Length 9in (23cm)
When Year-round
Where Island-wide
Habitat Woodlands, gardens, mangroves, parks

Although common throughout woodlands and gardens in Bermuda, the catbird is a species more often heard than seen. It is a slender, skulking grey bird which utters a distinctive cat-like 'mewing' call (hence the name) as it moves through the undergrowth.

Due to its furtive nature, this is a bird that is rather hard to see, despite being a frequent resident of Bermuda. A walk along one of the railway trails, or a trip to a local park, should reveal this species if you look carefully and keep your ears tuned. Although it has rather drab plumage, it is quite an attractive looking bird, with its black cap and chestnut feathers under the tail.

Bermuda White-eyed Vireo IX
Vireo griseus bermudianus

Common

Endemic sub-species

Alternative name(s) Chick-of-de-village
Length 5in (13cm)
When Year-round
Where Island-wide
Habitat Woodlands, gardens, mangroves, parks

This charming little bird is known locally as the 'Chick-of-de-Village' after its distinctive call (when you hear it, you'll realise why). A sub-species of the White-eyed Vireo, it is one of only two endemic birds in Bermuda - the other being the Bermuda Cahow - and is commonly found throughout the island in woodlands, gardens, mangroves and parks.

Like the Grey Catbird, it is often harder to see than to hear, but look out for its small olive and grey form as it flits through the trees searching for insects. It is best identified by its characteristic yellow lores (the area between beak and eyes) and obvious white eye-ring.

X Northern Cardinal
Cardinalis cardinalis

Introduced

Common

Alternative name(s) None
Length 8.5in (21cm)
When Year-round
Where Island-wide
Habitat Woodlands, gardens, mangroves, parks

This bright red bird is a common resident species, found throughout the island in woodlands and parkland. It is a large member of the finch family and was introduced to the island from North America in the 1800s. The males are easily identified, being scarlet in colour and having a prominent crest and black face. Females are browner than males, with reddish tints to wings, crest and tail. They have a large and formidable bill for cracking seeds.

Despite being an introduced species, the cardinal has apparently had little impact on the island's avifauna and for many Bermudians, is a welcome splash of colour to our woodlands.

3

AMPHIBIANS REPTILES & MAMMALS

Introduction

Wherever you go in Bermuda, you will spot reptiles. Brightly coloured Anolis lizards scuttle up walls or bask in the sun, the males wooing the ladies with their curious push-ups and displays. And although the endemic Bermuda Skink (the only native terrestrial reptile) is no longer found throughout the islands, you still have a chance to see it in Spittal Pond or on Nonsuch Island, sidling up to visitors for a quick lunch-time snack of left-overs. At sea, you might see Green Turtles. They used to breed in countless numbers, but are now only visitors. Keep an eye out in shallow waters for a glimpse of one coming up for breath.

During the warm Bermudian nights, the amphibians make their presence known. The Lesser Antillean Whistling Frog fills the air with its monotonous peeping, a noise that will either infuriate you or lull you to sleep; from a frog point of view, it certainly attracts the opposite sex! Throw in the low-pitched chorus of the Marine Toad and the night is filled with an amphibian cacophony.

Being a remote and tiny archipelago, Bermuda does not have any native land mammals and in the air, only a few bats make their way past on migration. However we are blessed with the presence of those most magnificent of sea mammals, the whales and dolphins. Between December and May, Humpback Whales pass the island on their way to the Northern feeding grounds, while pods of Bottlenose Dolphins use the waters around Bermuda to hunt and play all year round. You can look out for them from the shore, but to truly appreciate them, you will need to go on a boat tour.

Bermuda Skink I
Plestiodon longirostris

Endemic

Rare

Alternative name(s) Bermuda Rock Lizard
Length 6 to 7in (15 to 18cm)
When Year-round
Habitat Offshore islets, shoreline, coastal woodlands

The Bermuda Skink is our only endemic terrestrial vertebrate. This delightful, dark brown reptile moves swiftly over the ground in search of insect prey and, unlike the introduced *Anolis* lizards, is not found in trees. Bermuda skinks evolved in the large seabird colonies of ages past, where they would have scavenged on the remains of dead chicks and eggs. They are very curious and in areas where they are still found, they will inch closer and closer to picnickers in an attempt to scavenge any dropped morsels of food. This is one of the few endemics which you have a decent chance of finding, as there are isolated populations on the mainland at Spittal Pond, as well as on Nonsuch Island and other Castle Islands.

II Jamaican Anole
Anolis grahami

Introduced

Common

Alternative name(s) None
Length Males 7.8in (20cm) | Females 5in (13cm)
When Year-round
Habitat Everywhere!

The Jamaican Anole is our most common lizard and was originally introduced from Jamaica over 100 years ago to control fruit flies and cockroaches (both accidental introductions to the island). It swiftly colonised the entire island and is now found in most habitats, including our towns.

The male is predominantly greenish blue with a bright orange throat fan (called a dewlap), which it extends when attempting to attract the ladies. The female is smaller and greyish-green with an array of dark-edged diamonds down the centre of the back. These lizards can also change colour rapidly using specialised pigment cells called melanocytes which react to stress, making the creature look darker.

Antiguan Anole III
Anolis leachii

Introduced

Frequent

Alternative name(s) Leach's Anole, Warwick Lizard
Length 11.4in (29cm)
When Year-round
Habitat Gardens, woodlands

It is thought that this lizard, native to the islands of Antigua and Barbuda, arrived on our islands in the 1940s. Common to Warwick and Paget in particular, it is larger than the Jamaican Anole. The male has attractive green skin, liberally marked with blackish patterns, while its greyish head sports a golden eye. Its throat fan is a pale yellow colour. The females are smaller and more brownish, with a row of paler markings up the back. These lizards are not as common as Jamaican Anoles and spotting them requires a bit more time and patience.

Another introduced lizard to keep an eye out for is the Barbados Anole (*Anolis roquet*). These are larger, greenish-yellow lizards typically found on the West End of the island; you can identify the males by their pale blue-grey heads.

IV Diamondback Terrapin
Malaclemys terrapin

Native

Rare

Alternative name(s) None
Length Males 5.1in (13cm) | Females 7.4in (19cm)
When Year-round
Habitat Brackish water ponds, mangroves

There are two species of terrapin in Bermuda. The native Diamondback is by far the rarer of the two. Originating from North America and arriving naturally on Bermuda relatively recently (about 500 years ago), this species is now restricted to the ponds of the Mid Ocean Golf Course. Those playing a round of golf have the best chance of seeing one, although it won't be easy as numbers are low (recent population studies estimate around 100 individuals) and it is a shy species that lurks amongst the roots of mangrove trees. To learn more, visit the Bermuda Zoological Society website (www.bamz.org).

Our second terrapin, the Red-eared Slider (*Trachemys scripta elegans*), is rapidly colonising the island after store-brought pets were released into ponds. It is easily distinguished by the prominent red stripe behind the eye. Listed as one of the world's top 100 worst invasive species, the Slider eats our native Killifish and competes with the Diamondback for food and nest sites.

Green Turtle V
Chelonia mydas

Native

Frequent

Alternative name(s) None
Length 4.9ft (1.5m)
When Year-round
Habitat Coastal waters, open ocean

This is the most common marine turtle in Bermudian waters. Originally nesting in large numbers on our beaches, the appearance of the legendary shipwrecked settlers rapidly wiped out the breeding population. By 1930, the species had ceased to nest in Bermuda despite a law being passed as early as 1620 prohibiting their killing. However, the island's seagrass beds still provide important foraging areas for young turtles migrating from other areas, such as Cuba, Costa Rica and the US. Between 1968 and 1978 an attempt was made to re-establish a breeding population and thousands of eggs were buried on beaches of several offshore islands. Green Turtles are slow to reach sexual maturity so it takes many years for them to return to nest. There is still hope that one day they will once again be seen digging nest holes on our beaches, although sadly this has not happened yet. Sightings are not common but you may spot them off the coast, particularly in areas of dense seagrass.

VI Hawksbill Turtle
Eretmochelys imbricata

Native

Rare

Alternative name(s) None
Length 3.2ft (1m)
When Year-round
Habitat Coastal waters, open ocean

Even less common than the Green Turtle, the Hawksbill is also found in Bermudian waters. At first glance it looks a lot like the Green Turtle, but there are a couple of features to look out for that separate the two. The first is in the name; this turtle has a beak that is rather hawk-like compared to the blunter beak of the Green. Secondly, the scutes (or plates) on the turtle's back overlap, giving it a serrated look that is a bit saw-like. The Green Turtle on the other hand has a much smoother looking shell.

Unfortunately, the Hawksbill is currently listed as Critically Endangered, meaning it is on a fast track to extinction. This is because the species is still slaughtered illegally in some countries for its beautiful shell, which is often used to make cheap tourist trinkets; it is much better to see this amazing animal swimming free than turned into a useless souvenir. All turtles are legally protected in Bermuda and worldwide since 1981.

Lesser Antillean Whistling Frog
Eleutherodactylus johnstonei

VII

Introduced

Common

Alternative name(s) Coqui, Tree Frog
Length 1.3in (3.5cm)
When At night, year-round
Habitat Everywhere, but only visible at night

This diminutive frog is responsible for the monotonous 'peep peep' sounds that grace Bermudian evenings. Despite being heard most nights, few people actually see this species, which is tiny, brown and with a darker brown eye stripe over protruding eyes. Tiny suction cups on their toes help them clamber up walls and windows. To find one of these little frogs, the best bet is to walk around outside your hotel or guesthouse at night with a flashlight, paying special attention to windowsills and areas near foliage. Follow their call, which will cease abruptly when they realise you are nearby!

The Lesser Antillean Whistling Frog is yet another introduced species to the island, brought into Bermuda in the 1880s. It is native to a range of Caribbean countries. It is similar to a second introduced species, the Spalding's Robber Frog (*Eleutherodactylus gossei*) from Jamaica, which is much rarer and may even have disappeared from the island in recent years.

VIII **Marine Toad**
Rhinella marina

Introduced

Common

Alternative name(s) Cane Toad, Giant Toad
Length 5.9in (15cm)
When Year-round
Habitat Gardens, wetlands, ponds

Originally introduced to the island from Guyana in 1885, this species underwent a dramatic population explosion and is now common throughout Bermuda. Being the only toad species on the island, it is easily identified by its large size (much larger than the whistling frogs) and warty brown skin. It can be found in gardens, woodlands and, as it is able to swim in seawater, has even colonised some of our offshore islands.

Due to its occasional habit of consuming skinks (our only endemic reptile), and the fact that it possesses poison glands that can seriously harm or kill household pets, it is considered a pest species. Listen out for its low-pitched call, which has been likened to the idling of a diesel engine.

Humpback Whale IX
Megaptera novaeangliae

Native

Frequent

Alternative name(s)   None
Length   60ft (18m)
When   Mid-February to April
Habitat   Sea

This magnificent marine mammal can be seen in Bermuda as it migrates from breeding grounds in the Caribbean to summer feeding grounds near Greenland, eastern Canada and New England. It's a member of the Baleen suborder of whales and uses baleen (specially modified bristles) in its mouth to filter out krill and small fish from the vast amounts of seawater that it vacuums down its gullet. Humpbacks are also well known for their complex, beautiful songs that last 10 to 20 minutes but can in some cases extend for up to 24 hours. Once mercilessly targeted by the whaling industry (which also occurred in Bermuda), this species has been brought back from the brink of extinction by a worldwide moratorium on hunting in 1966. It can be differentiated from other whales and dolphins by the obvious hump of its back, the large black and white tail and the heart-shaped or bushy blow of its exhalation.

X Bottlenose Dolphin
Tursiops truncatus

Native

Rare

Alternative name(s) None
Length 6.6 to 13.1ft (2 to 4m)
When Year-round
Habitat Sea

Probably the best known dolphin species in the world – partly because it is unfortunately often kept in captivity – this is a large, grey dolphin with a distinctive forehead, stocky appearance and (you guessed it) bottle-like nose. Typically travelling in groups (or pods) of 10 to 30 individuals, they can occasionally come together in super pods numbering over 1,000. They are incredibly intelligent animals and are also highly social, communicating with each other via whistles and clicks that are audible to the human ear under water. Bottlenoses are equipped with rows of conical teeth and are very accomplished hunters. They target fish and squid for their supper. While not as commonly seen in Bermuda as our migratory Humpback Whales, you may see them on whale watching tours or, if you are extremely lucky, from the shore.

4

INSECTS
& CREEPY
CRAWLIES

Introduction

The insect world is the largest grouping of animals on Earth, with an estimated six to ten million different species, of which only a million have been as yet described. This represents an incredible 90% of all life forms worldwide! Despite being an exceptionally diverse group of animals, including butterflies, mosquitos, ants, grasshoppers and weevils, they all share the following characteristics: a chitinous exoskeleton, three pairs of legs, a three part body, a pair of antennae and compound eyes. Bermuda has its fair share of these fascinating creepy crawlies.

The other major grouping discussed in this chapter is spiders. While they may look like insects, they are actually air-breathing arthropods and differ from the basic insect body plan by having eight legs and no antennae. Lastly, to add an air of drama, we also throw in the centipedes; fast-moving, segmented predators with a ferocious bite.

Most of the species outlined here are relatively easy to see at close proximity (perhaps too close for comfort in the case of a few of the less visually pleasant species). So keep your eyes open around the hotel and in the garden. You never know what you are going to find out there!

Bermuda Buckeye Butterfly I

Junonia coenia bergi

Endemic sub-species

Common

Alternative name(s)   None
Wingspan   1.6 to 2.7in (4.2 to 7cm)
When   Year-round
Habitat   Gardens, woodlands, parks

Our only endemic butterfly (at the sub-species level), the Bermuda Buckeye is typically associated with Plantain and Capeweed, which often pop up as weeds on Bermudian lawns. The Buckeye is a medium-sized brown butterfly with prominent, multi-coloured eye spots on both the hind and forewings. The caterpillar is a small, black, furry looking beast covered with an array of black spines. Look for Bermuda Buckeyes in open sunny areas with sparse vegetation and bare ground. While the other sub-species of Buckeye Butterfly in North America is migratory, ours stay put on the island year round. Unlike some of our other endemic wildlife, you have a pretty good chance of seeing this beauty.

II Monarch Butterfly
Danaus plexippus

Native

Frequent

Alternative name(s) None
Wingspan 3.3 to 4.8in (8.6 to 12.4cm)
When Year-round
Habitat Gardens, woodlands, parks

The Monarch, one of our five common butterflies, is one of the most well-known and easily recognised butterflies in the world. This large, beautiful species is an orange colour with thick, black wing veins and a black body covered in white spots. The caterpillar is large with alternating stripes of white, yellow and black. Bermuda is host to some of the countless migrating Monarchs as they make their epic journeys in August-October to wintering grounds in Mexico and California. We also have our own resident, breeding population which is non-migratory and appears to have become established on the island after the original cedar and palmetto forests were opened up by early settlers. The caterpillars feed on plants of the Milkweed family so thoughtful Bermudians often grow this plant specifically for this butterfly!

Red Admiral III
Vanessa atalanta

Native (migrant)

Frequent

Alternative name(s) None
Wingspan 1.7 to 3in (4.5 to 7.6cm)
When Mainly spring and autumn
Habitat Gardens, woodlands, parks

The Red Admiral is a migrant to our island from the North American population (the species has a large world distribution, including Europe and Asia). It's actually pretty incredible to think of this fragile-looking insect making its way to Bermuda over the vastness of the open ocean. An attractive butterfly, the Red Admiral is black with a conspicuous reddish-orange band on both fore and hind wings, and pure white spots dappling the top of the forewing. Like many other butterflies, it prefers open sunny areas in gardens although it can also be found attending to flowering plants along the coast. It is partial to fermenting fruit.

IV Painted Lady Butterfly
Vanessa cardui

Native (migrant)

Frequent

Alternative name(s) Cosmopolitan
Wingspan 2 to 3in (5.1 to 7.3cm)
When Mainly spring and autumn
Habitat Gardens, woodlands, parks

The Painted Lady only visits our island. It is an orange-brown colour with darker brown wing tips and patterning, white or off-white spotting on the upper wing tips and dark brown dots along the edge of the hind wing. While it has been recorded feeding on over 300 different plant species, it is particularly fond of the nectar from species such as thistles, milkweed and privet. This butterfly is one of the most widespread of any in the world, being found in all continents except Antarctica and South America. As with the Red Admiral and the Monarch, this species is capable of migrating over large distances during the year as it follows the warmth (not unlike human visitors to Bermuda!).

Cabbage White Butterfly V
Pieris rapae

Introduced

Common

Alternative name(s) None
Wingspan 1.2 to 2in (3 to 5cm)
When April to September
Habitat Gardens, woodlands, parks, farmland

After the gaudy colours of our previous butterflies, the Cabbage White rather pales in comparison. This mainly white butterfly has delicate black forewing tips and black spots on the forewing (two in females, one in males). The caterpillar is pale green with a thin yellow line on its back. Introduced in the late 1800s, the Cabbage White has become quite a pest to local farmers as its caterpillar enjoys munching through cabbages (of course!). Indeed, the best places to see it are agricultural fields although it is also common in gardens.

VI Blue Dasher Dragonfly
Pachydiplax longipennis

Native

Frequent

Alternative name(s) Blue Pirate
Wingspan 2 to 2.3in (5 to 6cm)
When Year-round
Habitat Gardens, woodlands, parks

The Blue Dasher is one of the dragonfly species you are most likely to encounter in Bermuda. The males are particularly striking with their electric blue abdomen, white face and metallic green eyes. The females are a little less visually impressive, being dark brown with yellow stripes and having reddish-brown eyes. Dragonflies are accomplished predators, with both the adults and nymphs (young) ambushing and chomping down on other hapless insects. They really are fascinating to watch as they zip about at speed, their multi-faceted eyes searching for their next prey. Other dragonfly species in Bermuda include the migratory orange Wandering Glider (*Pantala flavescens*) and the bright red Vermillion Glider (*Tramea abdominalis*).

American Cockroach VII
Periplaneta americana

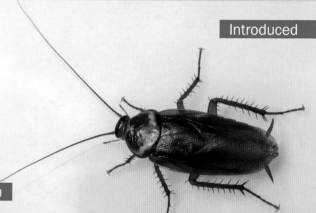

Introduced

Common

Alternative name(s) Various exclamations of dismay!
Length 1.5in (4cm)
When Unfortunately, year-round!
Habitat Unfortunately, everywhere!

This insect is a much reviled introduction to our island. Unfortunately cockroaches are a fact of life here in Bermuda and are often seen scuttling about in the kitchen (their running speed is equivalent to a human doing 210mph), or making a beeline through the air towards one's head with an unpleasant rustling of wings. It is important to note that seeing a cockroach in a house in Bermuda isn't a sign that the place hasn't been cleaned in a while (and I'm not simply making excuses here!), as our damp climate has proved optimal for this insect and it gets everywhere. They date back to the Carboniferous period so you have to respect cockroaches' ability to adapt and prosper with humans, something that can't be said for many other species. Another species of roach found on the island is the Surinam Roach (*Pycnoscelus surinamensis*). This burrowing roach is more uncommon and differs from the American Cockroach in being smaller and more bullet shaped, with a dark brown to black body and paler wings.

VIII **Spiny Orbweaver Spider**
Gasteracantha cancriformis

Introduced

Common

Alternative name(s) Crab Spider, Star Spider
Length Males 0.1in (0.3cm) | Females 0.4in (1cm)
When Year-round
Habitat Gardens, woodlands, parks

This small, attractive spider was introduced to Bermuda in the 1930s. It is quite distinctive, being white or pale yellow with black spots and several dark red or black spines protruding from its sides. It is this shape that gives rise to its other common names – the Crab Spider and the Star Spider.

The Spiny Orbweaver Spider can be seen in most terrestrial habitats, waiting patiently in its web, which is strung intricately across the branches of bushes and trees. Don't let those spikes fool you; this species is for the most part harmless to humans and, on close inspection, is rather attractive. It is not however harmless to the various flies and moths that find themselves ensnared in its webs, bound and cocooned as a tasty snack.

Golden Silk Spider IX
Nephila clavipes

Native

Frequent

Alternative name(s) Hurricane Spider, Banana Spider
Length Females 6in (15cm) | Males one-fifth the size!
When Year-round
Habitat Gardens, woodlands, parks

Also known locally as the 'Hurricane Spider', this large species is a native to Bermuda. They are a good way of forecasting the weather, as when storms and hurricanes are brewing, they spin their webs in lower, more sheltered locations. Women in Bermuda used to use the silken webs for sewing. The females are seen regularly throughout the island and are fairly fearsome in appearance (although they are harmless unless pestered, when they may bite in self defence).

Reaching six inches in length, they have long golden legs and a slender, delicately speckled body. The males are tiny in contrast and are only seen when attempting to mate, whereupon they cling hopefully to the female's web and, if they are lucky, copulate before being turned into a light post-coital snack...

X Giant Centipede
Scolopendra subspinipes

Uncertain

Frequent

Alternative name(s) St David's Centipede
Length 12in (30cm)
When Year-round
Habitat Gardens, woodlands, parks

Also known locally as the St. David's Centipede, this arthropod is truly worthy of respect. It can reach impressive sizes (up to 12 inches) and moves at great speed on its numerous legs. Its large, powerful jaws are capable of inflicting a painful bite, although this is usually a last resort and only if it feels cornered. It is an accomplished predator, eating anything it can catch and can even supplement its normal diet of insects with small mammals and birds. Although it is infrequently seen, it can be encountered throughout the island; look under stones in gardens if you dare! Just don't be tempted to touch them as they are aggressive and will attack if threatened.

The Bermudian antidote to a bite is to rub the wound with rum from a bottle with a centipede in it. A shot of good rum afterwards will probably have equal medicinal value!

5

FISH

Introduction

*B*ermuda's seas are alive with fish, making snorkelling a must when you visit. We have some of the most northerly coral reefs in the Atlantic Ocean, inhabited by darting, gem-like reef fish, while our open waters are the haunt of larger pelagic fish. Recent studies have yielded over 470 species around the islands, from large schools of tang to solitary lurking groupers, barracudas, brightly-coloured parrotfish and silvery bream. From a conservation point of view, many of these species are threatened by marine pollution, over-fishing, coral reef damage and, in recent years, the introduction of the Lionfish (Pterois volitans and Pterois miles), a highly invasive species from the Indian and Pacific Oceans that is a voracious predator.

Bermuda's reefs have also wrecked dozens of ships over hundreds of years, many of which are now diving attractions and home to marine creatures. They provide a fascinating insight into Bermuda's history. So get your swimsuit on, gear up with mask and snorkel, and have a look for yourself.

Those of you who don't want to get wet can also appreciate some of Bermuda's fish in rock pools, from the dockside or on one of our glass-bottom tour boats. Indeed, casting bits of bread or leftover lunch into the water can result in a piranha-like boiling of the sea as fish (such as bream and chub) fight over the morsels. And lastly, you can appreciate some of Bermuda's fish in our legendary fish sandwiches; just make sure you choose your fish from sustainable, locally-caught sources and those that practice dolphin, turtle and seabird-friendly fishing methods.

Bermuda Blue Angelfish I
Holacanthus bermudensis

Native

Frequent

Alternative name(s) None
Length 15in (38cm)
Diet Primarily sponges, but also jellyfish, corals, plankton
Habitat Reefs, inshore waters

A very distinctive species, the Bermuda Blue Angelfish is a delight to see as it swims gracefully around the reefs. It has a round body with matching, curved, yellow-tipped dorsal and anal fins that trail beyond the yellow-fringed tail. The predominant colour is cobalt blue, with fins edged a paler blue. In a case of 'stranger than fiction', this species is one of several fish that are capable of changing sex, with large females becoming males if there aren't many males in the population. Another angelfish often spotted in Bermudian waters is the Queen Angelfish (*Holacanthus ciliaris*), which is more boldly coloured, with yellow-edged body scales, a yellow tail, more patterning on the head and a prominent dark blue spot on the forehead.

II French Grunt
Haemulon flavolineatum

Native

Common

Alternative name(s) None
Length 12in (30cm)
Diet Crustaceans
Habitat Docks, reefs, inshore waters

The French Grunt is another common species, typically seen in large schools whilst on snorkelling excursions. This species has a yellow body with many horizontal silvery blue stripes. Found throughout Bermudan waters, grunts get their name by the curious noises they make by grinding their teeth and amplifying the sounds with their swim bladders. This sound can even be heard underwater.

Grunts are a common family, with other species including the Blue-striped (*Haemulon sciurus*) and White (*Haemulon plumierii*). For identification purposes between the various grunt species, look at the base colour, and the colour, number and width of body stripes.

Sergeant Major **III**
Abudefduf saxatilis

Native

Common

Alternative name(s) Cow Polly
Length 6in (15cm)
Diet Invertebrate larvae, small fish, algae, your leftovers!
Habitat Docks, reefs, inshore waters

This species is also known locally as the 'Cow Polly'. It is one of the most common fish you will see and can be found in a variety of locations, from just off the docks to rock pools and coral reefs. This large damselfish is easy to identify, with bold, black and white vertical stripes; the regimental stripes give rise to its military name. A vivid yellow wash covers the top of the body, which grades into a bluish-white below.

It is quite an inquisitive species and will swim unconcernedly around snorkelers, even approaching for a brief, painless nip. They are particularly aggressive when guarding their eggs, which they lay in patches and defend vigorously.

IV Rock Beauty
Holacanthus tricolor

Native

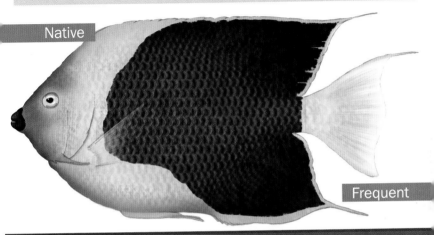

Frequent

Alternative name(s) Corn Sugar, Yellow Nanny
Length 10in (25cm)
Diet Sponges, jellyfish, corals, plankton, algae
Habitat Reefs, inshore waters

This stunningly beautiful fish is a member of the Marine Angelfish family and can be found off rocky shorelines or on coral reefs. Adults are bright yellow and black making them quite striking – so much so that they have even graced the 1979 'Bermuda Wildlife Definitive Stamp Set', making a grand appearance as the 40c stamp.

Pairs stay together year round and mate by rising up in the water, coyly touching bellies and releasing clouds of sperm and eggs. They can release a staggering ten million eggs in each spawning cycle, which then float off into the water column where the larvae are left to fend for themselves in the big blue world. Despite being relatively small fish, they are quite territorial and will make sudden and repeated rushes at snorkelers who venture too close. A belligerent but mainly painless nip for the unwary will often accompany this, so be respectful of their personal space!

Foureye Butterflyfish V
Chaetodon capistratus

Native

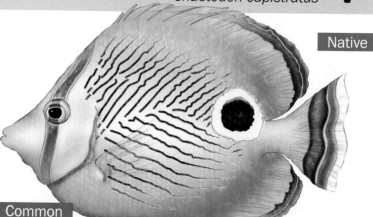

Common

Alternative name(s) Four-eyed Butterflyfish
Length 6in (15cm)
Diet Invertebrates
Habitat Reefs, inshore waters

Foureye Butterflyfish are often seen in pairs, circling their territories and defending them against any newcomers. These small fish have a laterally flattened body, which is yellow and white. The dorsal and ventral fins look like an extension of the body, and seem to blend into the tail, giving the fish a rounded appearance.

The two large, black 'eyespots', one on each side of the body near the tail, are used to confuse potential predators. This species can be easily seen in a range of our aquatic habitats.

Like the Rock Beauty, this species was also part of the Bermuda Wildlife Definitive Stamp Set.

VI Longspine Squirrelfish
Holocentrus rufus

Native

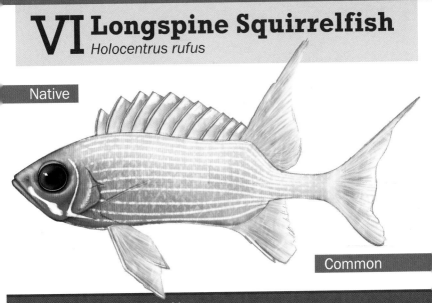

Common

Alternative name(s) None
Length 11in (28cm)
Diet Crustaceans, molluscs, gastropods
Habitat Docks, reefs, inshore waters

With its large eyes and red colouration, this is a readily identifiable species. Due to their predominantly nocturnal lifestyle, squirrelfish are usually found in rock crevices in the reef during the day. This species also has a prominent spiny dorsal fin that is capable of inflicting wounds when handled. As many a fisherman can attest, when caught on lines, their immediate response is to dive deep into a rock cavity, making extrication rather difficult. A second squirrelfish species, the Dusky Squirrelfish (*Sargocentron vexillarium*) is also commonly seen in Bermudian waters. It differs from the Longspine by being a deeper red colour with a goldish tinge and lacking the white tipping to the ends of the dorsal fins. Its second dorsal fin is also nowhere near as pronounced as in the Longspine Squirrelfish.

Great Barracuda VII
Sphyraena barracuda

Native

Rare

Alternative name(s) None
Length Up to 6.5ft (2m)
Diet Unwary fish
Habitat Open water, reefs

Although certainly not a commonly encountered species, the Great Barracuda will add a sense of drama to your diving expedition if you do spot one. This large, predatory species, which can attain lengths of up to 6.5 feet, certainly has an aura of menace about it. It has a long, sleek appearance, fearsome eyes and a very prominent series of large teeth. However, although it may attack if provoked, there have never been any recorded attacks on humans in Bermuda. This is a magnificent fish and can be quietly observed in the water while it goes about its business of hunting smaller prey. It does so by sitting motionless near the water's surface or around boats and moorings, before striking at unwary fish that pass haplessly nearby.

VIII Bermuda Bream
Diplodus bermudensis

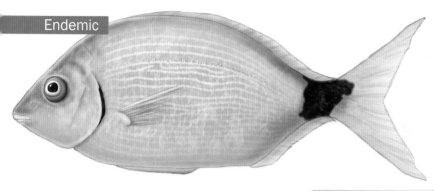

Endemic

Common

Alternative name(s) Bermuda Porgy
Length 12in (30cm)
Diet Invertebrates, any food you care to throw into the water!
Habitat Docks, reefs, inshore waters

Although not a species that is likely to 'wow' its audience with impressive colouration or a sleek appearance, the Bermuda Bream is one of our very few endemic saltwater species. They can occur in large schools off docks and in bays and will voraciously attack any floating bits of bread one may feel inclined to throw into the water. It is a dull grey fish with a rounded appearance and a small head. Another visually comparable species, the Bermuda Chub (*Kyphosus sectatrix*), can also be readily found in similar habitats, but differs in being a larger size, having narrow darker horizontal stripes on the body and lacking the black spot at the base of the tail.

Blue Parrotfish IX
Scarus coeruleus

Native

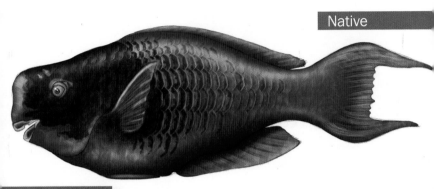

Frequent

Alternative name(s) None
Length Up to 35.5in (90cm)
Diet Algae on coral reefs
Habitat Reefs

Parrotfish are commonly seen throughout Bermuda and come in a variety of colours and sizes — at least 12 species in all. They can be rather confusing to identify, having several different colour phases as they mature from juveniles to adults. To make matters even more entertaining, they can also change sex and both males and females can look drastically different from each other. They play an important role in the reef ecosystem, using their specially adapted beak-like mouths (which gives them a parrot-like appearance - hence the name) to scrape algae off the surface of the reef. In parts of the world where coral bleaching has occurred, their numbers often increase dramatically as they feed off the profusion of algae that follows. Other parrotfish found in Bermuda include the massive Midnight Parrotfish (*Scarus coelestinus*), as well as the Stoplight Parrotfish (*Sparisoma viride*), Princess Parrotfish (*Scarus taeniopterus*) and Queen Parrotfish (*Scarus vetula*).

X Bluehead Wrasse
Thalassoma bifasciatum

Native

Frequent

Alternative name(s) Bluehead
Length 7in (18cm)
Diet Zooplankton, crustaceans, ectoparasites on other fish
Habitat Reefs, inshore waters

As you would expect, the male of this slender fish has a dark blue head. It is one of many wrasse species found in Bermudian waters and is certainly one of the most beautiful. While the females are rather drab, the males are patterned with the aforementioned blue head, a trio of thick black and white vertical stripes and a greenish body. Pairs of Blue-head Wrasses can often be seen in shallow waters, defending their territories and courting one another. As cleaner fish, they are important to the health of the reef. They also change colour depending on their social status and mating behaviour. Other wrasses found in Bermuda include the amusingly named Slippery Dick (*Halichoeres bivittatus*) and Puddingwife (*Halichoeres radiatus*), as well as the Bermuda Creole Wrasse (*Clepticus sp.*), the latter a recently recognised endemic to the island.

6

Introduction

Bermuda's underwater world is not just home to fish but also a wide range of strange and wonderful sea creatures. These range from the familiar lobsters and squid to the bizarre Upside-down Jellyfish, the 'look but don't touch' Portuguese Man o' War and the oddly beautiful but rather inactive Spotted Sea Hare. We've also included two fish species in this chapter, the Longsnout Seahorse and the Green Moray Eel, because their odd shapes and behaviours are better suited to this chapter. Don't let their atypical appearance confuse you though; eels are from the fish Order Anguilliformes while seahorses are in the Order Syngnathiformes (which includes other oddities like the pipefish).

You don't have to swim far off the beach to find many of these fascinating beasts. Some are easy to see every time you go for a dip; others are a challenge to locate, but are included because they are so intriguing. In some cases you don't even need to get into the water to encounter them, as several of these animals are found in rock pools along the seashore. Others, such as octopus, lobster and seahorse are much more challenging to find, particularly as they are masters of camouflage and spend a lot of their time sitting motionless in or near the reef surface. Of course, that just makes spotting one even more special!

As with all the other plants and animals described in this guide, please take care not to disturb them and leave them exactly as you found them. Some of them are extremely delicate and even the lightest of touches can negatively affect their health.

Longsnout Seahorse I
Hippocampus reidi

Native

Rare

Alternative name(s) Slender Seahorse
Length Up to 6in (15cm)
Diet Small shrimp, amphipods, fish
Habitat Reefs, shallow water, seagrass beds, rock pools

This diminutive resident of Bermuda's waters is unfortunately now quite a rarity and seeing one will require a lot of luck. It doesn't help that this incredible looking fish (and despite its appearance, it is indeed a fish) can change colours to camouflage itself against its background. Seahorses can be found in a variety of habitats, often quite close to the shoreline. They particularly like areas of seagrass in which to hide and anchor themselves using their prehensile tails. They have a bony, armour-like skin. Males have a smooth pouch on their bellies, which they use to brood the fertilised eggs. They also fight off other bachelors using an aquatic head-butt. Seahorses are becoming endangered the world over due to the tourist trade (where their desiccated bodies are stuck to tourist souvenirs), the aquarium trade and traditional Chinese medicines (sadly the cause of so many conservation problems worldwide). The Longsnout is particularly at risk because of its large size and bright colours.

II Green Moray Eel
Gymnothorax funebris

Native

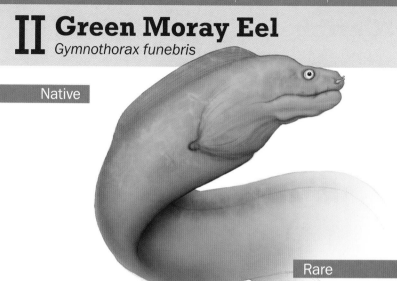

Rare

Alternative name(s) Black Moray, Green Conger
Length Over 6ft (1.9m)
Diet Unwary fish, octopus, invertebrates, fingers if poked!
Habitat Reefs

The mainly nocturnal Green Moray can be found from the shallows to the outer coral reefs, but they hide in rocky crevices and caves during the day, making them difficult to find. This species can reach impressive sizes of over six feet. With its length and sharp, pointed teeth, this eel can seem rather fearsome, especially as they open and close their mouths to push water over their gills to breathe, flashing those gnashers. As with most marine animals however, it will only bite if molested. The Green Moray doesn't have scales; rather, its body is covered in a yellow mucus, which looks green against the darker skin colour. When it catches prey that it can't swallow in one bite, it wraps its body around the fish to tear it into chunks; they can eat an octopus tentacle by tentacle. Other common morays in Bermudian waters include the Spotted Moray (*Gymnothorax moringa*; much smaller and spotted) and the Purplemouth Moray (*Gymnothorax vicinus*; much smaller, pale and finely speckled).

Caribbean Spiny Lobster **III**
Panulirus argus

Native

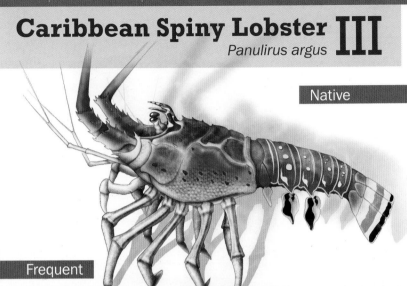

Frequent

Alternative name(s) Rock Lobster, Bug
Length 15.7in (40cm)
Diet Molluscs, chiton, small crustaceans, carrion
Habitat Reefs, shallow water

A crustacean that can reach impressive sizes, Caribbean Spiny Lobsters are a much favoured species for seafood enthusiasts and are thus protected in Bermuda throughout much of the year to prevent over-exploitation. They can be seen on many of our reefs, often quite close to shore, poking their two antennae cautiously out of rocky crevices. They are a predatory species and eat a variety of sea creatures, crabs and various shells (including young conchs). They are very active at night when they wander out to feed and scuba divers in the nocturnal world may be lucky enough to see these incredible animals as they roam along the sandy floors. They form annual aggregations to migrate across the Bermuda shelf as part of their mating cycle, creating what look like long lobster conga lines that cross the sea floor in the never ending quest for some lobster loving. As the young lobsters grow, they shed their exoskeletons and grow a new one; during this time they are particularly vulnerable to predation by large fish, sharks and octopus.

IV Sally Lightfoot
Grapsus grapsus

Native

Common

Alternative name(s) Red Rock Crab
Length Carapace up to 3in (8cm)
Diet Mainly algae
Habitat Shoreline, rock pools, reefs, shallow water

Many different crab species can be found along the Bermudian seashore, but the Sally Lightfoot is by far the most noticeable. A large red crab, it can be exceptionally fast moving, with rapid reaction times to possible predators, hence the name. You can often see several of these beautiful crustaceans scuttling over the rocks, browsing on seaweed and clinging tenaciously when a large wave breaks over them.

This species is easily spotted along the shoreline of Spittal Pond as it forages on the rocks. If caught by a predator, they can snap off their own limbs to escape, growing them back later.

Bermuda Land Crab V
Gecarcinus lateralis

Native

Frequent

Alternative name(s) Black-back Crab, Common Land Crab
Length Carapace up to 4in (11cm)
Diet Mainly vegetation
Habitat Shoreline, gardens, woodland

This land crab can be found in good numbers on dune systems or rocky shorelines, particularly along the South Shore. A stocky, medium-sized crab, it is a deep red in colouration with a darker purple back. It is a terrestrial crustacean and lives in burrows on land, often quite a distance from the ocean, only returning to the sea to spawn. Unfortunately the species has to negotiate our coastal roads as it heads towards the sea, with the result that large numbers fall victim to passing cars. This has drastically reduced the population. It is also the favoured prey of the Yellow-crowned Night Heron, which bashes its victims against rocks on the shoreline. Probably all you will see of this crab as you scour the shoreline, will be its scattered body parts.

VI Common Octopus
Octopus vulgaris

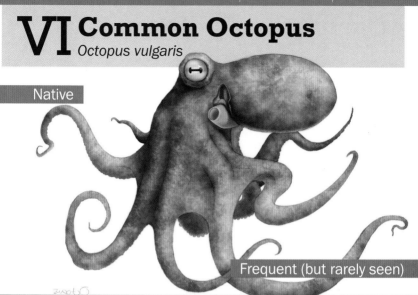

Native

Frequent (but rarely seen)

Alternative name(s) None
Length Mantle 10in (25cm) | Arms extending to over 3ft (1m)
Diet Crabs, bivalves, gastropods, fish, crustaceans
Habitat Reefs, shallow water, rock pools

The chances of finding an octopus are fairly slim, as they are shy creatures that are predominantly active from dusk into the night (although they do also hunt occasionally in the day, so keep your eyes open). You're most likely to spot them hiding under rocks, with perhaps just a couple of their eight arms showing and their large, strangely expressive eyes checking for predators. They can change their colour for camouflage. Their strong arms can grow up to three feet in length and are used for prising shells off rocks or holding unlucky crabs and lobsters while the octopus uses its beak to break their shells. They leave broken shells in "middens", so look for these little piles to find their lairs. They are also remarkably intelligent and have been shown to be easily capable of solving complex puzzles and mazes set for them by researchers. An octopus's life is short, usually between one and two years; they also have three hearts.

Caribbean Reef Squid VII
Sepioteuthis sepioidea

Native

Frequent

Alternative name(s) Cuttle, Scuttle
Length 8in (20cm)
Diet Small fish, shrimp
Habitat Shallow water, particularly near seagrass beds

In Bermuda, small schools of Caribbean Reef Squid can be seen near docks or over seagrass, scudding along backwards with their tentacles trailing behind them. They have huge eyes and are capable of very fast movements if they spot potential prey. The mantle of the Caribbean Reef Squid is a mottled brown colour, but the colours can darken or lighten depending on mood. They also use this colouration to communicate. If threatened, squid will release a dark cloud of ink into the water and then escape whilst their potential predators are disorientated. The squid are "semelparous", which means that they die after reproducing. While this squid is a tiny creature, the fathoms-deep waters off Bermuda may hold the Leviathan of the squid world, *Architeuthis dux*, the Giant Squid. A creature up to 60 feet long, and the inspiration for many tales about the Bermuda Triangle, this is not one that you will be seeing from our sun dappled shores as it prefers the endless night of the deep sea.

VIII Upside-down Jellyfish
Cassiopea xamachana

Native

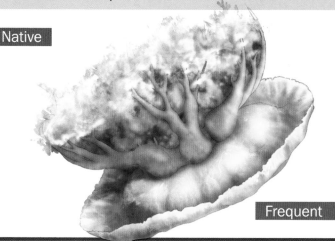

Frequent

Alternative name(s) Mangrove or Cabbage-head Jellyfish
Length Up to 12in (30cm)
Diet Filter feeds and catches small prey with its tentacles
Habitat Shallow water, particularly sheltered bays

These are remarkably odd jellyfish, usually found lying upside-down in groups on the bottom of the sea, looking rather like underwater flowers. They do this to expose algae on their tissues to the sun so that they can photosynthesise. The jellyfish then lives off the food that the algae generate. They also filter feed and can capture prey with their tentacles. Their umbrella is of variable colouration, being anywhere from a greenish to greyish blue, with its dense cluster of stinging arms facing towards the surface as it pulsates along the bottom of the shallows. They are capable of giving a painful sting, so be careful with them.

Upside-down Jellyfish can be found within inland ponds as well as inshore bays and mangroves with muddy or sandy substrates. They are vulnerable to pollution run-off from farms and urban areas. Walsingham Pond and Harrington Sound are good places to spot them.

Portuguese Man O' War IX
Physalia physalis

Native

Common

Alternative name(s) Jellyfish, Bluebottle
Length Float 12in (30cm) | Tentacles over 165ft (50m)
Diet Small fish, other marine organisms
Habitat Open water, shallow water, beaches (stranded)

This jellyfish is often found on Bermudian beaches, stranded on the sand. Normally an inhabitant of the open ocean, the Man o' War is actually a colony of animals called a siphonophore, each with its own special task. One animal is specially modified as a large purple-blue sail, which resembles an air-filled bag that the jellyfish uses to drift around the oceans. Other members of the colony are found in the long, trailing tentacles, which can stretch for tens of feet (in larger specimens, tentacles can reach more than an impressive 150 feet long). These tentacles are used by the jellyfish to sting, immobilise and kill its prey (normally small fish). This is also why one should never touch a Portuguese Man o' War; they can cause an incredibly painful sting, as many a local or tourist can attest. Even detached portions of tentacles can sting, so beware! The name comes from the 18th century Portuguese sailing ship, which looks a bit like the blue sail.

X Spotted Sea Hare
Aplysia dactylomela

Native

Frequent

Alternative name(s) Headache Fish, Sea Slug
Length 7in (18cm)
Diet Algae
Habitat Shallow water, shoreline, rock pools

Another fascinating beastie, the Spotted Sea Hare resembles a large brown sea slug with rather attractive black, ring-shaped spots covering the length of the body. It is sometimes known locally as the 'Headache Fish' due to the myth that it can cause headaches if touched — but we have no idea where that particular tall story came from!

It is a fairly common species in inter-tidal habitats where it grazes on algae. If disturbed it can release a stream of harmless purple dye, which rapidly dissipates in the water. They also have toxins in the skin which deters most creatures from eating them.

7

SHELLS & MORE

Introduction

Seashells have had a cultural significance for humans throughout time. We have used them as currency, tools, musical instruments and decoration. For the creatures that create them though, they are home, forming a defensive outer layer to protect them from predators.

Bermuda has a lot of fascinating shell species to discover. However, please note that many of these shells are protected by law, particularly in the case of the larger creatures; one should never collect shells if there are living animals inside.

As well as the seashells, this chapter includes some other Bermudian marine curiosities – urchins, chitons, anemones and sea puddings – along with the Bermuda Fire Worm and its flashy sexual exploits. You'll find many of these marine animals whilst exploring the seashore, whether amongst the rocky pools found at low tide near the beaches, or on our craggy, wave-splashed shores. Carefully turn over rocks and see what lurks beneath, or just stand still and observe what appears. We have many happy childhood memories of spending hours along the shore in St David's and Devonshire, poking about and marvelling at the many different animals that scuttled, crawled and scudded away. We hope that you will enjoy doing the same!

West Indian Top Shell I
Cittarium pica

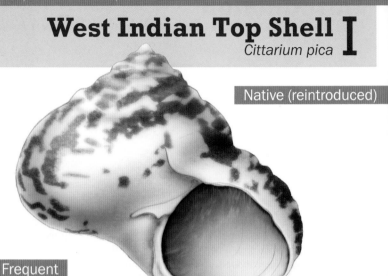

Native (reintroduced)

Frequent

Alternative name(s)   None
Size   Up to 5in (13cm)
Diet   Algae
Habitat   Shallow water, shoreline, rock pools

A protected species in Bermuda, this large marine snail was originally very common on our rocky shores. Their flesh was, however, widely sought after as a delicacy and the species was eventually wiped out due to over-enthusiastic collecting. It was subsequently re-introduced to the island in 1982 and 1989, when a small number of these shells were released on Nonsuch Island. Since then it has made a slow but steady comeback and can be found at various sites in Bermuda. It is a large, cone-shaped black and white shell, with black markings arranged in ragged spirals towards the apex.

II Harbour Conch
Strombus costatus

Native

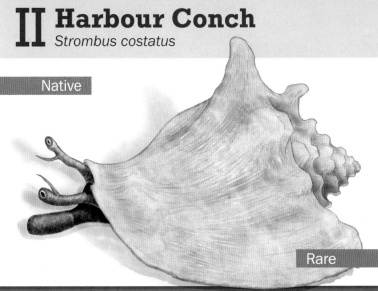

Rare

Alternative name(s) Milk Conch
Size Up to 8in (20cm)
Diet Algae
Habitat Shallow water, shoreline, beaches

The Harbour Conch is a large marine snail that has a thick, straw-coloured shell with a milk-white opening (hence its alternate name). Typically found in sheltered bays, conchs have been heavily harvested by humans in the past and their populations subsequently collapsed. They are now protected by law. Although the Harbour Conch has since slowly recovered, our other species, the Queen Conch (*Strombus gigas*), is still very rare. The Queen Conch is larger, with a more flared outer lip and prominent spikey protuberances, as well as sporting a pinkish opening. Hold an empty conch shell to your ear and you will hear the sound of the "sea", a curious effect caused by ambient noise resonating inside the shell's interior. Don't do this with a live one however, not least because of the blade-like foot, which is the primary arsenal in a conch's self defence! After humans, lobsters are thought to be their main predator. Conchs move in a leaping motion, whereby they extend their foot-stalk to lift the shell, then let it fall forwards.

Calico Clam III
Macrocallista maculata

Native

Rare

Alternative name(s) None
Size 1.3in (3.5cm)
Diet Filter feeders on plankton and fine particles
Habitat Shallow water, buried under sand

A very attractive bivalve, the shell of the Calico Clam is a pale coffee cream with numerous darker brown, square markings giving it a checkerboard effect. An edible species, it was once heavily harvested, resulting in a massive population decline. It has been protected by law since the 1970s and is now fairly common in some areas although its numbers have never recovered to historic levels. It can be found on sandy bottoms (particularly in Harrington Sound) where it lies slightly buried under the substrate. The Calico Clam is such a distinctive shell that you are unlikely to mistake it for anything else. It can also be found along the Atlantic coast of North and South America from North Carolina to Brazil.

IV Beaded Periwinkle
Tectarius muricatus

Native

Common

Alternative name(s) None
Size ½ to 1in (1.5 to 3cm)
Diet Mainly algae
Habitat Shallow water, shoreline, rock pools

These are small shells of the seashore and are very tolerant of being out of the water for extended periods of time; in fact, they don't like to be submerged for too long. The Beaded Periwinkle is the largest of our common periwinkles and is covered in small bumpy ridges. Often found in large concentrations, this sea snail has a thick and robust pale grey shell, beautifully shaped like a conical spire. Like other periwinkles, they are herbivorous, spending their days quietly scraping algae off hard surfaces in the intertidal zone.

Two other similar species in Bermuda are the Prickly Winkle (*Nodilittorina tuberculata*), which is smaller and more elongated with sandy, stripey markings, and the Zebra Periwinkle (*Echinolittorina ziczac*), which is smooth and covered in dark zigzags or stripes. The shells of all of these species are often taken over by hermit crabs after their owners have died and make handy new homes for these opportunistic little crabs.

West Indian Chiton V
Chiton tuberculatus

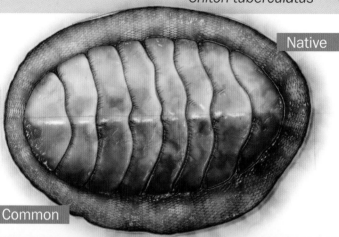

Native

Common

Alternative name(s) Suck Rock
Size Up to 3in (8cm)
Diet Algae
Habitat Shallow water, shoreline, rock pools

These curious snails have overlapping plates and cling tenaciously to the rocky shoreline, leading to the local name of 'Suck Rock'. They are exceptionally difficult to remove from their chosen spot, but closer inspection to the underside would reveal the dark body of the snail.

Like the periwinkles, this species spends its days methodically grazing algae off the rocks, moving imperceptibly along the littoral zone. Look for them in the intertidal area as they sit, stoically unmovable, while the waves crash into them. The separated plates of dead chiton are often misidentified as the teeth of parrotfish.

VI Green Sea Urchin
Lytechinus variegatus

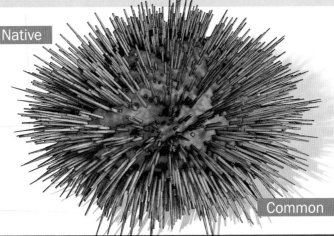

Native

Common

Alternative name(s) Variegated Sea Urchin
Size 4in (11cm)
Diet Seaweed, algae
Habitat Shallow water, seagrass beds, reefs, rock pools

Green Sea Urchins are a common resident of our seashores, rocky pools and reefs. Resembling a ball of sharp spines, this is a 'look but don't touch' species! Its colour varies from a light green to dark purple. It's often found with pieces of debris and algae stuck to its upper surface and held in place with its tube feet. This is thought to protect it from ultraviolet light in shallow water. Around its mouth it has an "Aristotle's Lantern" containing five teeth which it uses to scrape up food. Another two common species are the Rock-boring Urchin (*Echinometra lucunter*), which also has purple or deep red spines, and the White Urchin (*Tripneustes ventricosus*), which has short, thicker white spines. Both can be found further out on the reefs, where they trundle about feeding on various bits of vegetation and algae. Watch out for urchins when exploring the seashore as having their spines stuck in your flesh is not a pleasant experience.

Red Anemone VII
Actinia bermudensis

Native

Common

Alternative name(s)   Maroon Anemone, Stinging Anemone
Size   1.5in (4cm)
Diet   Whatever they can catch (small fish, invertebrates)
Habitat   Reefs, shallow water, rock pools

When walking along the rocky shoreline at low tide, you may occasionally come across what appears to be a small, red blob stuck to the rocks; this is actually a sea anemone. Once the tide rises and the sea encompasses the blob, little reddish to yellowish tentacles will emerge and the more familiar form of a sea anemone will take shape again. Relatives of corals and sea fans, sea anemones feed by catching small fish and other marine animals with their tentacles. They paralyse them with stinging cells (nematocysts) located on the tentacles and then shovel them into their mouths, which are located in the centre of the writhing mass of tentacles. There are several other species of sea anemone in Bermuda, including the Giant Caribbean Sea Anemone (*Condylactis gigantea*), which is larger and comes in a range of pastel colours, its tentacles tipped with purple, rose or green.

VIII Reticulated Brittle Star
Ophionereis reticulata

Native

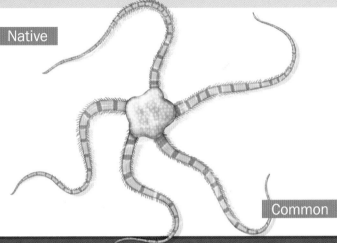

Common

Alternative name(s) None
Size Central disk 0.05in (0.15cm) | Arms up to 0.5in (1.2cm)
Diet Algae
Habitat Sandy sea floors, under rocks and boulders

The Reticulated Brittle Star is a curious looking starfish that is normally found on sandy sea floors or lurking under rocks and boulders. It has an intricately patterned, sand-coloured central disk, from which five brittle-looking arms arise. Each arm has pale brown bands along its length and is punctuated with short spines. It predominantly feeds on algae and other assorted detritus that it finds as it makes its way along the sea floor. If attacked by a predator, it swiftly detaches an arm in the hope of distracting the predator's attention onto the now separated limb for long enough to make a hasty bid for freedom. This process of limb detachment, called autotomy, gives the Brittle Star its name. Later on, the Brittle Star simply regenerates its missing limb and returns to business. Handy, eh?

Sea Pudding IX
Isostichopus badionotus

Native

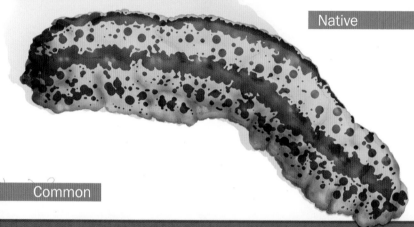

Common

Alternative name(s) Four-sided or Chocolate Chip Sea Cucumber
Size 11in (30cm)
Diet Micro-organisms from sand
Habitat Shallow water, seagrass beds

Sea puddings are curious, leathery-looking creatures and members of the sea cucumber family. They sit apparently motionless on the ocean floor, vying for the prize as one of the least exciting animals in the sea. Not one to invite to a cocktail party perhaps. Sea puddings come in a variety of fairly dull colours, from all black specimens to those that are pale brown with black blotches. Despite their inactive demeanour, they are actually very important members of the ecosystem, as they consume vast quantities of sand and efficiently strip it of various bacteria and micro-organisms. When disturbed (e.g. by someone picking them up for a closer look) they can occasionally expel their respiratory organs as white strands of a sticky glue-like substance. They regenerate these internal organs once the threat has passed.

X Bermuda Fireworm
Odontosyllis enopla

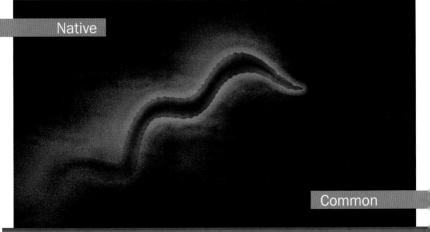

Native

Common

Alternative name(s) Bermuda Glow Worm
Size Females 0.08in (0.2cm) | Males 0.05in (0.13cm)
Diet Little is known
Habitat Shallow water, sand, rocks, seagrass beds

If you see the Bermuda Fireworm during the day, you might wonder what all the fuss is about. It's a tiny worm - reddish and covered in pale (and painful to the touch) bristles - but a worm nonetheless. Well, what gets people so excited about these beasts is their sex life. During the warm summer months, the Bermuda Fireworms all feel the urge to mate on the third night after the full moon, starting exactly 56 minutes after sunset. Females begin swimming up from the sea floor, bioluminescent with desire and making green, glowing little circles on the sea's surface. This acts as a come-hither call to all the males who immediately shoot up and into the glowing circle for a quick, flashy copulation. With so many worms merrily mating, the ocean is illuminated with sparks of green light. If you are visiting Bermuda during the summer, make sure you go and check out this incredible spectacle of nature; Ferry Reach Park is a great spot to do so.

8

FLOWERS

Introduction

Bermuda feels so lush and tropical thanks in part to its fabulous and exotic flowers, which provide welcome splashes of colour to our gardens and countryside. Although the majority of the flowers we detail below are not native to the country, many of them are an important source of nectar for our butterflies. Of course, that is what flowers are all about – providing an exuberant, brightly coloured flag to draw in pollinating insects. Butterflies and bees get nectar in exchange for doing this job, while the dusting of pollen on their backs or legs help the plants reproduce.

You don't have to go anywhere in particular to look for Bermuda's flowers. They are present just about everywhere, be it gardens, the roadside, parks or the shoreline; so take a second look at the hedge in the hotel or the bushes by the bus stop.

To get a more in depth knowledge, try the Bermuda Botanical Gardens, located in Paget. This 35 acre park was first opened in 1898, and contains a huge collection of plant species, from Bermuda and all over the world. There is even an aromatic garden for blind visitors. Take a picnic and while away at least half a day here.

Bermudiana I
Sisyrinchium bermudiana

Endemic

Frequent

Alternative name(s)   Blue-eyed Grass
Height   12in (30cm)
When   Blooms from April to June
Where   Coastal areas, sand dunes

This beautiful little purple flower is a Bermudian endemic and is also the island's National Flower. It can be found in a variety of habitats, from sand dunes to gardens, and blooms from April to June. While they may look a little like a grass, they are actually a member of the Iris family.

The Bermudiana is readily recognisable with its six purple petals, which are yellow at the base; it also has slender dark green leaves. It's a member of the Sisyrinchium genus, a large group of plants native to the New World.

II Hibiscus
Hibiscus rosa-sinensis

Introduced

Common

Alternative name(s) Chinese Hibiscus, China Rose
Height Up to 15ft (4.5m)
When Some varieties bloom year-round
Where Gardens island-wide

Possibly the most well known of Bermuda's flora, the Hibiscus covers Bermuda in a profusion of multi-coloured blooms. This much-loved flower is a common fixture in most Bermudian gardens and can range from dark reds to pinks and orange or pure white. It is originally from East Asia but is now found throughout the tropics where it grows well in the climate, needing little attention.

There are over 200 species of Hibiscus worldwide, and it has also been extensively hybridised. The flower is often seen tucked behind the ear of wandering tourists to give the wearer a tropical feel. We recommend it!

Oleander III
Nerium oleander

Introduced

Common

Alternative name(s) Pink Beauty, Laurier Rose
Height Up to 20ft (6m)
When Blooms in the spring and summer
Where Island-wide

Another popular garden shrub, often used to make bordering hedges, the Oleander is common throughout the island. It is easily recognised by its small white, pink or red flowers. This species was introduced to Bermuda from the Orient in 1790 and is an evergreen plant. A word of warning though; despite its beauty, all parts of this plant, but particularly the milky sap, are toxic and irritating. It's claimed that Alexander the Great had two soldiers die after using Oleander skewers to barbeque their meat, so beware!

IV Bermuda Easter Lily
Lilium longiflorum eximum

Introduced

Frequent

Alternative name(s) Bermuda Lily
Height 3ft (1m)
When Blooms late March and April
Where Look for in cultivated fields, gardens

Another species from the Orient, this time the Ryukyu Islands of Japan, the Bermuda Easter Lily is one of the island's best-loved flowers. This species produces beautiful, white, trumpet-shaped flowers between late March and April (the Easter period). The dark green leaves are a stark contrast to the pure white of the flower. It was once grown in huge quantities on Bermuda both for perfume, which was made locally, and also as an export. Up until the late 1800s, Bermuda supplied around 90% of the lily market in the US, usually timed to appear for Easter. The bulbs were packed in sand for transportation and the steamers could get the flowers to the mainland in 70 hours. The sales were of huge economic importance, but the majority of the industry died abruptly in 1899 when a virus destroyed the crop. It took almost 30 years for it to be identified. These days, a few small farms still grow this species for harvest in Bermuda. Traditionally, several blooms are sent each Easter to the Queen of England at Buckingham Palace.

Seaside Morning Glory V
Ipomoea pes-caprae

Native

Common

Alternative name(s) Beach Morning Glory, Goat's Foot
Height 2in (5cm), but can extend to lengths of 100ft (30m)
When Blooms year-round
Where Coastal areas

The Seaside Morning Glory is a common fixture of dune systems in particular. As with most *Ipomea* species, it is a sprawling vine with pale purple, trumpet-shaped flowers. There are eleven species of *Ipomoea* vine in Bermuda, but only three of these are native. Unfortunately, the most common one is the introduced *Ipomoea indica*, the Morning Glory or Bluebell, which tends to be reviled across the world due to its invasive nature. It can be found throughout the island and differs from the Seaside Morning Glory by having lilac flowers, which are larger and more funnel-shaped. Being a vine, Morning Glory can rapidly cover other plants and will ultimately smother them if left unchecked.

VI Poinsettia
Euphorbia pulcherrima

Introduced

Common

Alternative name(s) Crown of the Andes, Christmas Star
Height 2ft (0.6m) to 10ft (3m)
When Blooms from November to April
Where Island-wide

This attractive, deciduous shrub is particularly prevalent at Christmas when potted Poinsettias provide festive colour to Bermudian houses for the season. It has tiny golden flowers at the centre of large, specially modified red or white leaves (known as bracts). There are many different varieties including "Red Glitter", "Pink Lipstick" and "Strawberries and Cream". This species is originally from Mexico and Central America but is now common throughout the tropics. It was named after Joel Poinsett, a US Ambassador to Mexico who introduced the plant in the mid 1800s. The plant only blooms when the days get short enough to provide 14 hours of darkness. Bermuda does have a native poinsettia too, the Joseph's Coat (*Poinsettia heterophylla*) which grows in parks and nature reserves. If you are on the island at Christmas time, be sure to check out the traditional Poinsettia flower display at the Bermuda Botanical Gardens – it is always stunning!

Common Lantana VII
Lantana camara

Introduced

Common

Alternative name(s) Spanish Flag, Sage
Height 3ft (1m)
When Blooms year-round
Where Island-wide

The Common Lantana, also known as Sage, is an invasive, evergreen shrub found in many parts of the tropics and is common throughout Bermuda, having been introduced before the 1800s from the Bahamas. It is readily identifiable by its profuse clusters of small flowers. These can come in a range of pastel colours, from red to yellow, orange to white, with the clusters consisting of random combinations of colour. An attractive plant, it is an important nectar species for butterflies. The leaves emit a strong, characteristic odour when crushed between the fingers (although this species is not edible). It will out-compete native plants if allowed to grow free because the leaves are poisonous to most herbivores, while the berries are eaten by birds, which further spread the plant.

VIII Bird-of-Paradise Flower
Strelitzia reginae

Introduced

Frequent

Alternative name(s) Crane Flower
Height 6.5ft (2m)
When Blooms year-round
Where Island-wide, predominantly in gardens

It doesn't get more tropical or exotic than this! The Bird-of-Paradise, or Crane Flower, is an incredible looking plant. The flower head, which emerges from a large horizontal and specially adapted leaf, consists of a series of orange and blue petals which resemble the crest, head and beak of a bird. In its native South Africa, this plant is pollinated by several species of sunbird (the African version of hummingbirds, except their wings don't whirr!).

Bird-of-Paradise can be found in gardens throughout Bermuda.

Common Passion Flower IX
Passiflora caerulea

Frequent

Introduced

Alternative name(s) Blue Passion Flower
Height 10-20ft (3-6m)
When Blooms year-round
Where Island-wide, especially in gardens

A South American species, *Passiflora caerulea*, is one of several passion flowers found locally in Bermuda. Its name comes from Spanish and Portuguese priests, who considered the flower to represent the crucifixion. The 10 outer flower petals represented the apostles present at the Crucifixion, followed by 72 darker filaments representing the crown of thorns, 5 anthers for the wounds and 3 styles representing the nails. Lastly, the coiling tendrils, which the plant uses to bind itself to supporting structures, are supposed to be the whips. Religious imagery aside, this is a beautiful purple flower which can be used to make perfume and is important to insects. It produces an orange, edible fruit (not as tasty as the purple passion fruit though).

X Royal Poinciana
Delonix regia

Introduced   Frequent

Alternative name(s) Flame Tree, Flamboyent, Peacock Flower
Height 50ft (15m)
When Blooms in July and August
Where Botanical Gardens, gardens island-wide

Another favourite for tourists and locals alike, the Royal Poinciana is found throughout the island. Its magnificent, bright red flowers, which typically bloom in July and August, wreath the tree in crimson colours, giving rise to another of its common names - the Flame Tree. The leaves are compound, between one and two feet long and are rather fern-like in appearance.

This tree, which can reach heights of 50 feet, is a native of Madagascar but is now widely distributed throughout the tropics. It's a legume, which means it has nitrogen-fixing properties and is good for the soil. It also provides excellent shade.

9

TREES & SHRUBS

Introduction

Bermudians have relied on trees and their many products ever since people first set foot on the island. Cedars were cut down to build the celebrated 'Deliverance', the vessel used by the shipwreck survivors to finally escape from the island and continue the journey to North America. More wood was used to create houses and furniture.

St. Peter's Church in St. George's is a fine example of this. It dates back to the 1620s (the oldest Anglican church in the Western Hemisphere in use outside the British Isles) and has priceless, ancient cedar beams and a carved, red cedar altar thought to be the oldest piece of woodwork on the islands. Sadly, many of our cedars died during the infamous Cedar Blight and the trees are now protected by law; local artisans use wood from dead trees to make high quality products such as hurricane lamps and sculptures.

Over time, introduced species have made their way into the ecosystem, in some cases entirely changing the landscape. In areas where forests of Bermuda Palmetto and Bermuda Cedar once stood, the land is often blanketed with near mono-cultures of Fiddlewood, Mexican Pepper and Allspice. The change has been dramatic and now much of Bermuda looks vastly different from the island that the shipwreck survivors found.

Some of these trees, such as Loquats and Surinam Cherries, provide a pleasant fruity treat when we walk along quiet woodland trails, while the shade of various palm trees enable us to sit on the beach in comfort as we contemplate the ocean. So next time you are resting under the shade of a tree, watching the ocean sparkle in the distance, have a closer look and see if you can put a name to it. With this book in hand, hopefully you will!

Bermuda Cedar I

Juniperus bermudiana

Endemic

Frequent

Alternative name(s) Bermuda Juniper
Height Up to 50ft (15m)
Where Island-wide, but try Ferry Reach and Nonsuch Island

The obvious first entry to this chapter — the Bermuda Cedar — is our most famous endemic tree. Prized for its beautiful smelling, reddish-coloured wood which graces most old Bermudian houses, this evergreen was once the dominant tree in our woodland areas. It was especially useful for shipbuilding as it was resistant to rot and woodworm and was lighter than Oak. The berries were used to make a cure for coughs. Sadly that all changed between 1946 and 1953, when the accidental introduction from America of two species of scale insects spread a cedar blight throughout the island. This lead to the demise of 95% of Bermuda cedars, and the forlorn dead trunks of these trees still haunt many of our hillsides. Luckily a very small number of these trees were resistant to the devastating effects of the blight and over time, these individuals have been propagated and some areas replanted with blight-resistant trees. This species can once again be found throughout the island, although the cedar forests of old are unfortunately a thing of the past

Male cedar trees have yellow, cone-like flowers and females have blue-grey berries.

II Bermuda Palmetto
Sabal bermudana

Endemic

Frequent

Alternative name(s) Palmetto, Bibby-tree
Height Up to 82ft (25m)
Where Island-wide

Just as ubiquitous in pre-settlement forests as the Bermuda Cedar, the Bermuda Palmetto was historically our second dominant tree species and was also relied upon heavily in ages past. Bermuda Palmetto fronds were used as thatch and for the making of hats and rope while the fruit was ground into flour. However, this species was not as heavily affected by over-exploitation and disease as the beleaguered Bermuda Cedars and is still a frequent sight on the island, although it suffers from competition with introduced species. This salt tolerant plant is the only endemic species of palm on the island and all other similar species, such as the Chinese Fan Palm (*Livistonia chinensis*), are introduced. Settlers also made a strong alcoholic drink, known as 'bibby', by drilling into the tree to extract the sap and fermenting it; nowadays visitors tend to stick to 'Dark n' Stormies,' a tasty island cocktail made with Barritt's Ginger Beer and Goslings Black Seal Rum.

The Palmetto has clusters of tiny yellow-white flowers and a small, dark fruit.

Bermuda Olivewood III
Cassine laneana

Endemic

Frequent

Alternative name(s) Olivewood Bark
Height Up to 43ft (13m)
Where Island-wide, but try Blue Hole Park

The last of the endemic trio in this chapter, the Bermuda Olivewood was another key species in the pre-settlement era and would have been found scattered about the cedar- and palmetto-dominated woodlands. Its bark was used for tanning leather in early settlement times. It is a bushy, evergreen tree that can grow over 40 feet high and, when flowering, produces clusters of small yellowish-white flowers. Although not a common species anymore, this tree can be found in many of our parks and gardens. To see it, along with cedars and palmettoes, visit Blue Hole Park - where several specimens have been planted along the main paths - or Spittal Pond.

IV Red Mangrove
Rhizophora mangle

Native

Frequent

Alternative name(s) None
Height Up to 80ft (24m), but typically only 20ft (6m)
Where Hungry Bay, Blue Hole Park, Paget Marsh

The Red Mangrove, and its counterpart, the Black Mangrove (*Avicennia germinans*), are the only species of mangrove in Bermuda. Typically, Black Mangroves are found on the landward side and Red on the coastal side. Both species can also be found in inland ponds. The main identification pointer to tell these species apart is their root systems. The Red Mangrove has large prop roots, which emanate from the main trunk into the surrounding water. The Black Mangrove has many small blunt roots (pneumatophores) sticking out of the mud. Look too at the seed of the tree; Black Mangroves have a large, round seed whilst the Red has a smaller seed with a long, brown-tipped root. These seedlings germinate while attached to the parent plant. Once they fall into the sea, they can float on the currents for a year or more before they take root. Mangroves protect coastlines from the power of the sea, act as nursery areas for fish and can protect reefs from muddy waters and pollutants. They have pale yellow flowers and small brown fruits.

Casuarina V
Casuarina equisetifolia

Introduced

Frequent

Alternative name(s) Australian Pine, Horsetail Tree, Ironwood
Height Up to 116ft (35m)
Where Island-wide

The first of our introduced species to make it into the Top 10, the Casuarina tree is one of the most obvious of the island's tree species. Originally from Australia and the Pacific region, it was introduced in the 1950s to compensate for the catastrophic loss of endemic Bermuda Cedars after the cedar blight. It quickly took hold on the island and spread far and wide. It is covered in long, thin, green needles, which produce a dense blanket under the tree and prevent anything else from growing. This completely alters the understory ecosystem, with negative impacts on both flora and fauna. The tree produces spikes of tiny, reddish-brown flowers and round, woody, berry-like fruits with sharp edges that are painful to step on.

In some areas, this species is now being removed to make way for blight-resistant Bermuda Cedars again.

VI Bay Grape
Coccoloba uvifera

Native

Common

Alternative name(s) Seagrape
Height Up to 32ft (10m)
Where Island-wide (particularly in coastal areas)

A more recent native arrival to the island, it is thought that the Bay Grape probably reached Bermuda only slightly before our first settlers. It is highly adapted to life on the coast and can tolerate the extremes of this environment, from salt spray to heavy sea winds. A medium-sized tree, it has large, flat, round waxy leaves and, starting in late summer, is covered in clusters of berries that turn from green to purple as they ripen (hence the name Bay Grape). These berries are often made into jam, which is well worth trying! The species is commonly found in our coastal environments and is unique enough that it is unlikely to be confused with any other species. People sometimes clip these trees into a hedge to form a windbreak.

Fiddlewood VII
Citharexylum spinosum

Introduced

Common

Alternative name(s) None
Height Up to 50ft (15m)
Where Island-wide

One of the most common tree species on the island, the Fiddlewood was introduced from the West Indies and quickly became naturalised around the island. It is a fairly large species, standing up to 50 feet tall, and produces a small white flower. It has been remarkably successful since its introduction and now dominates much of our woodlands. Another common introduced species is the Allspice (*Pimenta dioica*) whose leaves produce a strong spicy smell when crushed in the hand. Unlike the Fiddlewood, which drops its leaves in early summer, this tree retains its leaves year round and the flowers are small and white. Both of these species will be easily seen whilst you wander our woodlands.

VIII Match-Me-If-You-Can
Acalypha wilkesiana

Introduced

Frequent

Alternative name(s) Copperleaf, Jacob's Coat, Tricolor
Height Up to 8ft (2.5m)
Where Island-wide, particularly in gardens

The Match-Me-If-You-Can is an introduced shrub that is a native of the Pacific Islands. Now commonly found in Bermudian gardens, often as part of a border hedge, it can grow up to 8 feet high and spread out more than 6.5 feet. It is so named because it is apparently impossible to find any two leaves that are exactly alike in pattern; if you've got time on your hands, give it a go if you don't believe us! The leaves are an attractive mix of purples, bronze and green. You should come across this species when walking in any of our towns or neighbourhoods. Look for its fuzzy catkin-like flowers; these are the male flowers. Each shrub also has female flowers with smaller spikes that generally remain hidden amongst the leaves.

Surinam Cherry IX
Eugenia uniflora

Introduced

Common

Alternative name(s) Brazilian Cherry, Cayenne Cherry
Height Up to 26ft (8m)
Where Island-wide, but try Walsingham and Blue Hole

Another vigorous introduction, the Surinam Cherry can form dense, monoculture stands of trees. A good example of this is in Walsingham, where much of the original forest has given way to a dense Surinam Cherry grove. This species has small, light green leaves and can fruit several times a year. It produces a small, red-ridged fruit, which is quite sweet when ripe and is actually rather tasty; they should be a deep, bluish-red and fall right off the tree when you pick them. They are high in vitamin A and C, but don't eat the seeds. Several shops also sell local Surinam Cherry jam; give it a try!

X Loquat
Eriobotrya japonica

Introduced

Frequent

Alternative name(s) Japanese Medlar
Height Up to 32ft (10 m)
Where Island-wide, particularly in gardens

The introduced Loquat tree is found throughout Bermuda and is medium-sized with large, dark-green leaves. It produces a sweet, yellow fruit between February and April. This fruit, packed with vitamin A, is much loved by locals and tourists alike and can be eaten straight off the tree or turned into jams, pie fillings and chutneys. It can also be used to make a loquat liqueur. Introduced to the island from Japan in the 1850s it is now a common fixture in gardens and towns.

10

NATURAL PLACES

Introduction

Now that you have read about all of these amazing animals and plants, it's time to go and find them. Despite its small size and the fact that Bermuda is the third most densely populated place in the world, the island has some wonderfully wild areas dotted throughout the country, many of which have been legally protected.

In all, there are 13 Nature Reserves, managed by the Bermuda Department of Conservation Services. These protect hundreds of hectares of the island's natural beauty. The Bermuda National Trust and the Bermuda Audubon Society also manage important habitats. Both inside and outside these protected areas you can find pristine beaches, secluded bays, dense woodlands, hidden grottos, rugged cliffs and primeval marshes.

A great way to visit many of these sites is via the Bermuda Railway Trail; the railway is long gone, but you can walk, ride or cycle almost the entire length of the original route (18 of the original 22 miles). You'll need to divert off the trail to visit these reserves, but that's part of the fun. It will give you a great insight into what Bermuda's wildlife is really all about.

Nonsuch Island I
Castle Harbour, St. George's Parish

Woodland

Marshes

Shoreline

Beaches

Sea

Size 14 acres (5.7ha)

What You'll see loads! White-tailed Tropicbird, Bermuda Cahow nesting sites, Bermuda Skink, Green Turtle, West Indian Top Shell, Bermuda Palmetto, Bermuda Cedar

One of the most important wildlife sanctuaries in Bermuda, Nonsuch Island is the largest of a group of islands located at the mouth of Castle Harbour in the East. It was named after Nonsuch Castle in Surrey, UK, built by Henry VIII in 1538 and reputed to have no equal. Over the years, it has been a yellow fever quarantine hospital, a training school for delinquent boys and a research station. Nowadays, it exists as a 'Living Museum' to preserve native plant species and keep at bay the hordes of introduced species. As well as important plants, the island contains a healthy population of rather tame Bermuda skinks. A project to bring nesting Cahows back to Nonsuch had its first success in 2009 when a chick hatched on the island for the first time in 400 years. Each year has seen the numbers of these rare, endemic birds increasing and it is hoped that in the future it will once again be dotted with the burrows of these special seabirds. Nonsuch can only be visited by permit from the Department of Conservation Services (www. conservation.bm).

II Great Head Park
St. David's, St. George's Parish

Woodland

Shoreline

Beaches

Sea

Size 24 acres (9.7ha)
What You'll see White-tailed Tropicbird (from the cliffs), Grey Catbird, Bermuda White-eyed Vireo, Jamaican Anole, Silk Spider, Fiddlewood, Casuarina, Humpback Whale

Great Head Park is the largest park in St David's and offers an extensive trail system that winds its way through dense woodland and leads out onto spectacular cliffs overlooking the sea (although be warned that many of the trails are overgrown). It also encompasses St David's Battery, with its two massive breech-loading guns (built in 1910) pointing defiantly out to sea. The cliffs by the battery are a great spot to look for White-tailed Tropicbirds, as well as Humpback Whales at the right time of year (mid-February to April). A short distance from Great Head Park is Cashew City, a small local beach with shallow waters and at low tide, lots of interesting rock pools. This beach is far removed from the more touristy beaches of the South Shore and is a favourite for St David's locals. If you want to keep exploring, you can also follow another trail that leads away from Cashew City along the rugged shoreline towards the remains of an old fort (this is only accessible at low tide and disappears at high tide).

Tobacco Bay **III**
St. George's, St. George's Parish

Shoreline

Beaches

Sea

Size Small, but packed with interest!

What You'll see too much to list! White-tailed Tropicbird, Great Kiskadee, Blue Parrotfish, Blue Angelfish, French Grunt, Sergeant Major, Common Octopus and many others

Tobacco Bay is a hidden gem in St George's. It was apparently named after shipwreck survivors from the *Sea Venture* found tobacco growing here in 1609, possibly planted earlier by the Spanish or Portuguese. Only a 30-minute walk from the town centre up Duke of Kent Street and over the hill, the rocky outcrops around the beach offer excellent snorkelling opportunities and the many rock pools can provide hours of exploration for adults and children alike. There's also a café, bar and restrooms. The bay itself is a really safe and sheltered swimming area suitable for the whole family. Following the unusual limestone outcrops around from Tobacco Bay leads to the sheltered, shallow environs of Coots Pond. The muddier substrate of the bay and fringing mangroves provide a different snorkelling experience to the sandy floors and reefs of Tobacco Bay. Further round the corner lie Achilles' Bay and Fort St Catherine Beach (where the first weary shipwreck survivors landed).

IV Ferry Point Park
Ferry Reach, Hamilton Parish

Woodland

Shoreline

Beaches

Sea

Size 64 acres (25.9ha)
What You'll see White-tailed Tropicbird, Grey Catbird, Bermuda White-eyed Vireo, Jamaican Anole, Crab Spider, Bermuda Fireworm, Bermuda Cedar, Casuarina

Also known as Ferry Reach Park (the old ferry operated from here), this is a large and lightly wooded section encompassing a series of old fortifications, a Martello Tower (a defensive, circular fort resistant to cannon fire, usually with a moat and an artillery piece on the roof which could fire 360°) and several small islands overlooking the North Shore. The railway trail leads to Ferry Reach and the whole area is covered by a series of paths that take in the small beaches and protected coves. It's great for both naturalists and those interested in the more historical aspects of Bermuda's heritage as well as being the site where the spectacular mating displays of the Bermuda Fireworms take place in the shallow waters around one of the islets (see Chapter 7). During the summer, at 56 minutes after sunset on the third night after the full moon, the waters are transformed by the mesmerising green light trails of the fireworms as they perform their mating ballets. Well worth watching if you are in the neighbourhood!

Walsingham Nature Reserve V

Blue Hole Hill, Hamilton Parish

Woodland

Caves

Shoreline

Beaches

Sea

Size 12 acres (4.9ha)

What You can find Grey Catbird, Bermuda White-eyed Vireo, Northern Cardinal, Green Turtle, Mangroves, Bermuda Cedar, Surinam Cherry, Fiddlewood, Yellow Wood

Incorporating Blue Hole Hill Park and Idwal Hughes Sr. Nature Reserve, Walsingham encompasses a fascinating area of woodland and shoreline. You will find the start of this park system just after you cross The Causeway from the town of St. Georges. Although much of the woodland is composed of introduced species (specifically Surinam Cherry, Mexican Pepper and All-Spice), there are small pockets of Bermuda Cedar and Palmetto, along with Olivewood and Yellow Wood. The wonders of this area are the many hidden caves, grottos and lagoons which appear unexpectedly, some interconnected by a series of underwater cave systems. Two quick words of warning though: (i) keep an eye out for Poison Ivy, which grows in some parts of the reserve and causes painful skin irritations and rashes, and (ii) don't enter too far into the cave systems themselves, as they are fragile ecosystems and can also be quite dangerous!

VI Spittal Pond
South Shore, Smith's Parish

Woodland

Marshes

Shoreline

Beaches

Sea

Size 64 acres (25.9ha)

What Look for White-tailed Tropicbird, Yellow-crowned Night Heron, Moorhen, Sally Lightfoot, Bermuda Skink, Bermuda Cedar, Casuarina, Olivewood

One of Bermuda's premiere nature reserves (and, at 25.9 hectares, also its largest), this wetland is recognised as being internationally important by the worldwide Ramsar convention. Spittal Pond itself is a wide, brackish pool ringed with salt marsh and mud flats and is home to a large diversity of migratory wildfowl and waders, along with a resident colony of Yellow-crowned Night Herons. The rugged shoreline is good for spotting White-tailed Tropicbirds from February to October. Although not guaranteed, you have a fair chance of seeing Bermuda Skinks here. There's also an interesting limestone pavement formation called the "Checkerboard". Portuguese Rock boasts the earliest evidence of human presence on the island, with the inscription 'RP' and the date 1543; it is thought to have been made by Portuguese sailors and probably stands for Rex Portugalis (King of Portugal) suggesting they intended to claim Bermuda for Portugal. The rock itself has been replaced with a bronze casting of the inscription to prevent further damage.

Arboretum VII
Middle Road, Devonshire Parish

Woodland

Gardens

Size 22 acres (8.9ha)
What You'll find Mourning Dove, Grey Catbird, Bermuda White-eyed Vireo, Jamaican Anole, Silk Spider, Spiny Orbweaver Spider, as well as many flowers, trees and shrubs

Although not strictly a natural area, the Arboretum in Devonshire Parish is close enough to Hamilton to allow visitors to wander among the groves of trees after a day's shopping in our capital. Within the 22 acre site, there are several small glades and rocky areas to explore, dotted with native and exotic species like rubber and ebony from all over the world; some were given by Queen Elizabeth II from the Kew Garden collection. Further into the Arboretum is a densely wooded area, which also has several trails. During migration periods, and in the winter, the area provides some good bird watching moments. It is home to the Deputy Governor, whose official residence is in the southwest corner of the park. The Arboretum is the wild version of the Bermuda Botanical Gardens in nearby Paget, which is also well worth a visit to see many of the flowers, trees and shrubs mentioned in this guide.

VIII Paget Marsh
Middle Road, Paget Parish

Woodland

Marsh

Size 25 acres (10.1ha)
What You'll see Yellow-crowned Night Heron, Moorhen, Grey Catbird, Bermuda White-eyed Vireo, Silk Spider, Red Mangrove — and a wide range of rare marsh plants

Paget Marsh is a large Bermuda Palmetto and Bermuda Cedar marsh (and also contains our only freshwater Red Mangroves), jointly owned by the Bermuda Audubon Society and the Bermuda National Trust. This 25 acre site is the perfect way to step back in time to when the first settlers arrived on the island, as the swampy environs are exactly what they would have encountered over 400 years ago. Sadly most of Bermuda's marshes have long since been destroyed, by landfill and agriculture, and this remnant is therefore one of our most important protected areas. Although the majority of this marsh is inaccessible, one section has been opened up to the public by way of a boardwalk, allowing access to the heart of the marsh. A series of interpretation boards enhance the experience, and one can get good views of a variety of marsh plants not readily seen elsewhere on the island.

South Shore Park **IX**
South Shore Road, Southampton Parish

Shoreline

Beaches

Sea

Size 1¼ mile (2km) long

What Keep an eye out for White-tailed Tropicbird, many of the fish and sea creatures outlined in this book, Bermudiana

Most visitors to Bermuda will end up at Horseshoe Bay, arguably our most famous beach. As with many beaches in Bermuda, Horseshoe Bay has a strikingly pink hue to the sand. This is caused by the remnants of millions of 'foraminifera'; tiny, dark-red, single-celled animals that grow along the underside of Bermuda's coral reefs. As the reddish skeletons of these animals break down in the wave action and mix with particles of shells and corals, beautiful pink sand is formed. However, the crescent-shaped expanse of Horseshoe Bay is only a small part of this fabulous park. This area has a long ribbon of sand dunes, sparingly covered in shoreline vegetation, linking secluded coves and inlets, such as Stonehole Bay and Jobson's Cove, and ending at Warwick Long Bay. While the azure seas are great for swimming and snorkelling and the pink sprawling beaches tempt sunbathers, make sure you take a little time to explore the area more fully as there is so much more to see. This park also provides ideal views for photographers.

X Hog Bay Park
Middle Road, Sandy's Parish

Woodland

Farmland

Shoreline

Beaches

Sea

Size 32 acres (12.9ha)
What Look for White-tailed Tropicbird, Yellow-crowned Night Heron, Grey Catbird, Bermuda White-eyed Vireo, Spiny Orb-weaver Spider, Bermuda Cedar, Casuarina, Bay Grape

In Sandy's Parish lies Hog Bay Park, a large area criss-crossed by nature trails. It was named after the herds of wild pigs dropped off by Spanish sailors to help out anyone who ever got shipwrecked here (with catastrophic impacts for native wildlife). A leisurely walk along these trails initially takes you through fertile agricultural land, consisting of small fields scattered amongst the woods. Some will have been farmed since the 17th century and are still growing broccoli, salad and potatoes. There is also an ancient limestone kiln close to the car park. The path eventually leads to the sea, via a hillside covered in Bermuda Cedars, both live specimens and those killed off by the cedar blight. The expansive view of the ocean is stunning, a gradation of blues leading off to the horizon. Hog Bay Beach, located at the western end of the park, is a good place to relax (at low tide only). Due to the difficult terrain, you'll probably end up with the place to yourself. The seagrass beds are ideal for snorkelling. During migration, this is a great area for bird watching.

there's just a sense
by David F. Raine

there's just a sense that Nature lives in an unreal world of words;
of green and smell and unfurling leaves;
of perfume, blues and pinks.

there's just a sense that Nature lives in a world of petals, twigs and gold;
of pollen, bees and honey, stamen, furs, and seeds.

there's just a sense that Nature lives in the eyes of us who look;
and in the feel of finger tips and the smells which taunt the nose.

and there's just a sense that Nature lives where no man dares to go;
along the windy, darkened paths and among the damp mangroves.

there is a sense that Nature lives with a bird upon the wing;
in the calling of a treefrog, and in the voice of those that sing.

there is a sense that Nature swims, in the sea with whales, and fish, and porposies;
in the coral reefs, and shrimps.

and surely there is Nature too in the cries of the Cahow;
in the footprints of crabs on sandy beaches and the gentle lapping of the waves.
there's a sense that nature lives, above us everyday;
it's there along the narrow lane, and in the air we breath;
it was there the day that we were born
and will be there when we leave.

Written April 1992, Bermuda
Amended by André F. Raine, April 2009, Malta

André F. Raine

Dr. Raine is a Bermudian ornithologist who has worked on conservation projects throughout the world. He spent his youth exploring the rocky coastlines and tide pools of St. David's Parish. While undertaking his BSc in Wildlife Biology in Canada, he returned each summer to work as part of the government's Conservation Unit, becoming an expert on the island's wildlife. He also spent several years helping with conservation efforts to recover the population of Bermuda Cahow - one of the world's rarest seabirds - and became the second person to successfully hand-rear an abandoned Cahow chick to fledging. His MSc thesis focused on Bermuda's only endemic terrestrial vertebrate - the Bermuda Skink. He has a PhD from the University of East Anglia on moorland birds and has written three bird books, including The Photographic Guide to the Birds of Bermuda, and numerous scientific publications. He currently runs an endangered seabird project in Hawaii.

Helen Raine

Helen Raine has an MSc in Conservation and has worked as a Conservation Officer for Natural England UK and a Project Manager for the EU LIFE Yelkouan Shearwater Project with BirdLife Malta. She has undertaken fieldwork in England, Malta, Peru, Zambia and Hawaii, often living for months in a tent. Her adventures in bird ringing and conservation continue to take her around the world. As a freelance journalist, she has published hundreds of travel articles on adventure destinations for inflight magazines and travel supplements. She writes on a diverse range of subjects for newspapers including the Times of Malta and 'Pink', a women's magazine.

Find her work at www.helenraine.com.

Jill Raine

Bermudian Jill Amos Raine is a teacher, artist and former gallery owner. A watercolourist, Jill has been honoured on various occasions; her work was presented to royalty, including Queen Elizabeth II, Princess Anne, Princess Margaret and also Margaret Thatcher. She was chosen to represent the country in Carib Art, and has has exhibited as a Bermuda Biennial artist four times, in 1994, 2002, 2006 and 2008. Recently, she was Grand Marshall for the Bermuda Day Parade and a participant in Bermuda's "World Intellectual Property Day" celebrations. She was selected as the Artist in Residence in Breckenridge, Colorado in 2011. Originals and prints may be purchased directly from Jill or from several Bermuda galleries.

See her work at www.bermudamade.com/jill-raine

Jason Raine

Jason is an art director and scientific artist who specializes in biomedical visualization and 3D animation. His illustrations have appeared in pre-eminent science textbooks for high schools, post-secondary and medical schools across North America. His work in 3D animation has been used to educate physicians, nurses, scientists and patients across Europe, Austalia and North America, and has been awarded numerous international awards in healthcare education and marketing.

My work on this book is dedicated to my wife Anna and our beautiful children, Madeleine and Kingston. May your lives forever be filled with curiosity and wonder.

NOTES

NOTES